Man and Woman among the Azande

Sir Edward Evan Evans-Pritchard, M.A. Oxon, Ph.D. London, F.B.A., was born in 1902 the second son of the late Rev. Thomas John Evans-Pritchard and was educated at Winchester, and Exeter College, Oxford, where he was an honorary Scholar. From 1926 to 1939 he made six major and several minor anthropological expeditions to Central, East and North Africa. From 1926 onwards he held a series of high academic posts in both foreign and English universities, including being Professor of Social Anthropology at the University of Oxford from 1946 to 1970. He was a fellow of All Souls and was Sub-Warden of the college from 1963 to 1965. In 1971 he was knighted. He wrote several important anthropological studies including *Essays in Social Anthropology* and *The Position of Women in Primitive Societies and Other Essays in Social Anthropology*.

He died in September 1973.

Man and Woman among the Azande

edited by

E. E. EVANS-PRITCHARD

*Professor Emeritus
in the University of Oxford*

FABER AND FABER
3 Queen Square
London

First published in 1974
by Faber and Faber Limited
3 Queen Square London WC1
Printed in Great Britain by
Butler & Tanner Ltd, Frome and London

ISBN 0 571 10407 x

© *Professor E. E. Evans-Pritchard, 1974*

Contents

PREFACE   9

PART I · OLD TIMES

HUSBANDS AND WIVES   19
Children resemble their parents · Sperm · Begetting a child ·
Intercourse with a small girl · Conception · Child in the
womb · Birth · About giving birth · Habits of midwives ·
Babies' food · A man and his newborn baby · Marriage ·
Marriage of an elder · Bridewealth · Divorce · Marriage and
divorce · Marriage · Taking a wife · Marriage to boys · A
matrimonial problem · Meals · A wife puts food away for her
husband · A man's admonishment to his wife · Barrenness ·
Women's work and men's work · What wives dislike ·
Woman's work · The murder of Ngbandia · Husband and
wife · A man and his wife and his wife's family · Burial
alive of widows · Plaints · Widows

FAMILY, KIN AND IN-LAWS   75
Orphans · Habits of elders · Blessing · Cursing · Journeys
and ghosts · Porterage and the ghosts · Death and a girl
child · Mother's brother—sister's son · A girl at her
brother's home · Parents-in-law · A boy and his paternal
aunt · A maternal uncle's wife · A man and the son of his
elder brother · Kinship · Relationship terms · Grandmother ·
In-law behaviour · Mother-in-law · About myself (Tito) ·
Camp · Men address the ghosts at their nephew's shrine · A
maternal uncle's curse · Wives of sons mock the corpse of
their father-in-law · A mother-in-law addresses the ghosts
at her son-in-law's shrine · Women erect a shrine · An
old woman's admonishment of her son's wife · Suicides ·
children and sex · Incest

LOVERS AND ADULTERERS   109
Youth and girl · Love affairs · Making love · About
woman · Dances · Youth and maiden · A woman mourns

5

Contents

her lover · Youths chat among themselves · The cheating of
love affairs · Women are stupid · A dream · Lesbianism ·
Man and woman · A typical case about adultery · Adultery ·
A man and a woman: an adultery case · Mutilation · The
mutilation of Gbitarangba · Vengeance · A scandal · Men
converse on a path · Bad habits of men

PART II · MODERN TIMES

PREFACE   141

HUSBANDS AND WIVES AND LOVERS AND FAMILIES   143
Division of bridewealth · Husband and wife (about meat) ·
Husband and wife (about huts) · Husband and wife (about
cultivating) · A second wife · Husbands and wives · Wives
and husbands (two women converse) · A court case · Man
(Dingiso) and wife (Nabaatu) in cultivations · The wives of
Bagu and Sendego · Zamai, his wife Nakaya and their little
son Toro · A tale: a husband and yam peel · A tale: a mother
and daughter · About a witch-doctor's dance · About cotton
clothes · Widows · Father and son (about cultivating) · Talks
in the home on family affairs · Mother and daughters · An
old man talks to his sons about past and present · How the
young men lived · Wealth · Jealousy among an elder's wives ·
Helping elders in their cultivations · Some features of Zande
life today · Homesteads of married men · Visiting in-laws ·
Settlements in the past · Visiting relatives · A man and his
sweetheart in his hut · Youth and girl at a dance · Girls talk
about men · Love affairs · Two women gossiping

INDEX   197

Illustrations

1. Two girls   *facing page*   94
2. Boys' circumcision dance   94
3. Young girls   95
4. Women beating Eleusine for a Feast   95
5. Youths   110
6. Assembly for Prince Rikita's Feast   110
7. Daughters and wives of Prince Rikita   111
8. A man mutilated for adultery   111

Preface

In 1937 I published a book about the Azande people of Central Africa: *Witchcraft, Oracles and Magic among the Azande*. Then came the war and I could no longer for many years write about this people. I have recently been able to return to my Zande studies. A book on their folklore, *The Zande Trickster*, was published in 1967 and a further book, *The Azande; History and Political Institutions*, in 1971. I should now write books on their family and kinship life, and also on their religious thought and ritual, but *vita brevis*.

All I want to do in this small book is to introduce to a European audience in a series of sketches what Africans, or at any rate some Africans, are really like, how they talk and think; and with only the barest introduction and commentary. It has seemed to me that anthropologists (include me if you wish) have, in their writings about African societies, dehumanized the Africans into systems and structures and lost the flesh and blood. It may be somewhat of an experiment, but in these texts I am asking Azande to say in their own way what they want to say. The texts are on a variety of topics, but all are in some way or another concerned with relations between men and women, and domestic life.

The first draft of this book was very much longer than its present length. It is hoped that those texts which have been cut out can be published in book form on a future occasion. The reduction in size has also meant that the choice of which texts to include and which to exclude has had to be highly selective and even to some extent arbitrary. Some further reconstruction was also found desirable. The texts in Part I were taken down orally by me, or sometimes by my clerk Mr. Reuben Rikita, from illiterate Azande between 1927 and 1930. Those in Part II were written by Mr. Richard Mambia and Mr. Angelo Beda in the years 1961 to 1964. In the first draft these different sets of texts were combined under the headings of various topics but on further consideration I came to the conclusion that, so many changes having taken place in Zandeland between the two periods, the reader who had not visited Zandeland in either period might easily have become confused. Consequently they are now presented separately.

It will be appreciated that the form of presentation adopted imposes severe restrictions on the impresario, if I may so describe myself. The texts do not follow each other in a strictly logical order, nor were they taken down to do so; there are repetitions, and also what may seem irrelevancies (they were not to the Azande who dictated or wrote them), but were I to attempt to organize them the purpose of this exercise would be defeated. I must add that I cannot be held responsible for the sexual content in some of the texts. The relationship between men and women is often in part a physical one; and in any case I did not elicit the texts—love-making is a major Zande interest, from one point of view or another, almost an obsession it may appear to some.

This is, beside being a presentation of an African way of reflecting on how men and women see one another, a contribution to that problem of how men and women get along together in any part of the world. It does not attempt to solve it—perhaps it cannot be solved—but merely to tell, in their own way of telling it, how an African people look at it.

When I was in Zandeland I perhaps felt on the whole on the side of the men rather than of the women, though I knew that the women suffered discriminations. They were undoubtedly inclined to be what, as these texts will show, the men gave them to be. If I now tend to lean to the other side it is with reservations, for the texts demonstrate that the men are not entirely to blame; though I ought to add that all the texts in this collection were taken down from men, who naturally had a bias in their own favour. And if we may be inclined to pass judgement on the Zande male for his attitude to his womenfolk should we not remember that the battle for women's rights in Britain is only just over, if indeed it is; and should we not recollect that the great Aristotle in his *Politics* mentions women only to compare them with slaves, the male being by nature superior and the female inferior—the one rules and the other is ruled? And what have the world religions taught us in this respect? Moreover, though in the past women had only a nominal voice in selecting their mates and were sometimes treated more or less as chattels, they could stand up for themselves if need be. A wife unjustly used could always appeal to her husband's kin, her

Preface

own kin, and the prince, an appeal the husband was likely to find embarrassing, especially as the wife, to make her case the more impressive, might insert into it innuendoes which cast doubt on the husband's virility. Then she had always the weapons of refusing to sleep with him, refusing to cook for him, and a general and prolonged sulk; and if he attempted to punish her she could, and did, go back to her parental home and he might find it difficult to persuade her father to insist on her return—he, in the meantime, being unable to maintain his home by himself, especially in the preparation of meals, having to leave his home and stay with kinsfolk in his humiliation and discomfort. I think that all this comes out quite clearly in the texts.

Many of the texts recorded here have appeared elsewhere, often in the vernacular as well as in translation, and I make acknowledgement to the Clarendon Press, Faber and Faber, Routledge and Kegan Paul, Mouton, and the Oxonian Press (and All Souls College), and to the editors of *Sociologus*, *Anthropological Quarterly*, *Sudan Notes and Records* and *American Anthropologist*. A register of the vernacular texts is in preparation. I have had great help in preparing this book for publication from Miss Juliet Blair, and I make acknowledgement to the Social Science Research Council for my having been able to have her assistance.

Before saying anything more I must pay my respects to B. Malinowski, who was the first to impress on me the importance of recording texts in the vernacular among primitive and illiterate peoples. It was, I believe, impressed on him by the Egyptologist Sir Alan Gardiner. It is true that one is then confronted with a problem. Editors of journals look at one with frozen horror when presented with texts in a little, or entirely, unknown language; and subsidies for private publication are hard to obtain. I have done what I can. I can do no more.

Publication of texts in the vernacular gives the reader confidence that the anthropologist understood the language he claims to have understood. The fieldworker will find it invaluable to have recorded most of his notes in the vernacular when, like me, he has had to wait many years before he has had the opportunity to make public his records. He will find that, however long the lapse of time, his mind is back where it was then, that he is able to think in the language of the past. He can take a flight back through time. But what is most important, I think, about recording texts in the vernacular and then giving a faithful rendering of them in English, is that by doing so one allows the native to speak for himself, give his point of view without the anthropologist interrupting and, as he think, being an interpreter. There is much in these texts which the anthropologist might be inclined to cut out as irrelevant to the theme he fondly believes he is pursuing; but such remarks and comments, and to us, perhaps, seeming asides, are not irrelevant to the native, or he would not have said them; what he said was significant to him; and that it was significant to him should mean that it is significant to us.

These texts were taken down by my hand between forty and fifty years ago. In those days there were no tape-recorders, it had to be done the hard way. I did not solicit the topics of the texts and I have faithfully recorded what I took down, adding nothing and taking away nothing. I have even avoided comments on the texts, except where absolutely necessary. Such commentary as might be thought to be required is now provided by the very considerable literature on the Azande (a bibliography of which is attached). If there is some sex-talk in the texts, I did not introduce it; food, sex and witchcraft are constant themes in all these relations, and understandably so. Some of the nuances may be missed by those who do not know the Azande and their language. Azande often say one thing when they mean another.

This and other difficulties in translation may be mentioned, but this is not the occasion to discuss them. The reader may notice a certain inconsistency of style in the translation of the texts. This may be partly due to the fact that I have been translating them for more than twenty years, and my own rendering of Zande into English may have changed a little over the years; and I can indeed now think of some improvements in some of the renderings, but as most of the texts have already been published, here and there, in the vernacular with translation I am bound in the main to adhere to those translations. A translator is, in any case, always open to criticism for making his translation too literal or not literal enough. But the inconsistency, or apparent inconsistency, is due, I think, rather to the fact that there are different speech-styles in Zande, according to the situations in which speech is spoken, and these have therefore to be presented in somewhat different styles in English. Furthermore, the texts were taken down from different people, and everyone has, up to a point, his individual style, so there can be, if one is to stick to the sense given to his words, and the manner in which he presents them, by each narrator no absolute conformity in translation. A final word—the translation of Zande, tenses and genders in particular, involves considerable problems into which I do not think this is the place to enter. They would require linguistic treatment, which I hope to devote to them elsewhere. In this matter, as in others, I do not wish to make excuses, but I may perhaps be allowed to say that had not political difficulties cut me off from my Zande friends some phonetic and semantic problems might more easily have been solved.

Since this book was written a friend, Professor Lucy Mair, has been kind enough to read it in typescript and make some comments on it. It seemed to me to be a bore to have to write another introduction, having already written three, to books on Zande life, but she insisted that though I may have written much about witchcraft and other topics elsewhere it does not follow that the reader of this book will have read what has been written, so therefore to obey her instruction I add a few words on certain matters.

The notion of witchcraft is on almost every page of the book, as it is on the lips of Azande every day. Whether they are right or wrong is not for me to say, but so it is. Almost every misfortune for a Zande is due to witchcraft. There are various moves they can make to be rid of it. In the first place they can locate the witchcraft by consulting oracles. These are rubbing a sort of board to see whether it sticks or not; putting sticks into termite-mounds to see which will be gnawed; and, most important the giving of what we would regard as a poison to chickens to see whether they live or die in answer to a question. Having, by one or other of these means, discovered the witch who is causing the Azande trouble, usually sickness, they ask him to blow out water to show his goodwill and withdraw his malice, if any, which he will do. It follows that as misfortunes of one sort or another are frequent so are feelings about witchcraft, and also accusations towards close neighbours, those between whom and the sick and injured there could have been animosity. Should a man die his death is attributed to witchcraft and magic is made to avenge him.

I am also taken to task by Professor Mair for not having sufficiently explained what amounts to, or used to amount to, a Zande marriage. What happens, or used to happen, is that a man gave some twenty spears, bit by bit, to the father of a girl to take her as his wife. In general this worked quite simply. A gave spears to B, and B passed them on to C for a marriage to his son. In other words a daughter left the family and a daughter came into it. Naturally there was a good deal of bargaining but for this book no further comment is required. It was just like that.

Then a few words may be said about the bond of blood-brotherhood which comes frequently into the texts. This was in the past (it would not appear to be today) a very strong relationship between a man and his friend. By drinking each other's blood, a custom common in Africa, men undertook to help each other in every circumstance under penalty of death if they did not do so. It made a kind of kin-relationship where there was no kinship.

Finally, Professor Mair insists that I say something general about *sanza* since this notion, either overt or hidden, runs throughout the texts. This is a very difficult problem. I have translated the word as 'double-talk', but there is much more to it than that. We all hide our thoughts behind words but it seemed to me, and Azande themselves say so, that a Zande very often is deliberately evasive and obscure in his talk in order to say what he wants to say without actually saying it, even to the point of saying the opposite of what he means. This sometimes has made translation of the texts difficult.

The literature on the Azande is considerable. The main publications about them are listed below:

CALONNE-BEAUFAICT, A. DE, *Azande*, Bruxelles, 1921.

CZEKANOWSKI, JAN, *Wissenschaftliche Ergebnisse der deutschen Zentral-Afrika Expedition 1907–8 unter Führung Adolf Friedrichs, Herzog zu Mecklenburg*. Bd. 6, 2: *Forchungen im Nil-Kongo-Zwischengebiet*, Leipzig, 1924.

EVANS-PRITCHARD, E. E., *Witchcraft, Oracles and Magic among the Azande*, Oxford, 1937.

— *Essays in Social Anthropology* (Chapters 5–9), London, 1962.

— *The Position of Women in Primitive Societies; and other essays in social anthropology* (Chapters 4–8), London, 1965.

— *The Zande Trickster*, Oxford, 1967.

— *The Azande: History and Political Institutions*, Oxford, 1971.

'GERO' (GIORGETTI, F.), *La Superstizione Zande*, Bologna, 1966.

— *Death among the Azande of the Sudan*, Bologna, 1968.

Preface

HUTEREAU, A., *Histoire des peuplades de l'Uele et de l'Ubangi*, Bruxelles, 1922.

LAGAE, C. R., *Les Azande ou Niam-Niam*, Bruxelles, 1926.

LARKEN, P. M., 'An Account of the Zande', *Sudan Notes and Records*, Vol. IX, pp. 1–55.

— 'Impressions of the Azande', *Sudan Notes and Records*, Vol. X, pp. 85–134.

REINING, CONRAD, *The Zande Scheme*, Illinois, 1966.

SCHLIPPE, PIERRE DE, *Shifting Cultivation in Africa: the Zande system of agriculture*, London, 1956.

Part I
OLD TIMES

Husbands and Wives

CHILDREN RESEMBLE THEIR PARENTS

When a person bears a child, the child's face may resemble its mother's, and its legs may resemble its father's; so people say, 'look at that baby there, he is like his father and also his face is like that of his mother.' So Azande say about it that the souls of a wife and her husband unite to produce a child, for a baby is begotten who resembles both its mother and its father. So say the Azande.

SPERM

The first time a boy gets an erection with sperm in clearing a way in his penis it may trouble him while it makes a way. When it happens and he for the first time ejaculates sperm it is hot for him like fire. After that he begins to ejaculate coolly. The first sperm just comes like water for a long time, for about three months, then real sperm begins to come. Then the lad begins to ejaculate sperm properly. He really ejaculates sperm, sperm which is like an egg, and quite cool.

BEGETTING A CHILD

Azande say that a small boy has not sufficient sperm to beget a child. He must first grow and his inside first press for his sperm to be ready for begetting a child.

A man who copulates with his wife when she is far gone in pregnancy may spoil his child's mouth with his penis.

INTERCOURSE WITH A SMALL GIRL

In the past when a girl was small she did not copulate with men, thinking that she would not have intercourse with her husband because, since she was not developed, if she got with child how could she bear it since her hole [vagina] would not be big enough. She thought it were better the man should mount between her thighs. But today even a small girl knows all about intercourse with men. This is something new.

CONCEPTION

However much intercourse a small girl has her mucus is not capable of giving her a child. It is only after her breasts begin to grow and her hips broaden and strengthen that her mucus begins to contain souls of children. The mucus which a girl excretes shortly after her first intercourse is like water. Thus Azande say that a girl must grow up before she can have a child. If she conceives before she is properly grown up she will die in childbirth. This is why a man will not think his wife barren because she does not bear him children when she is small, but he waits till she is grown up, and it is only when her breasts have begun to fall without her having given birth to a child that her husband begins to think that she is barren.

CHILD IN THE WOMB

When a woman is pregnant and the child is already strong in her body, then all the foods she eats, the young child eats his in the juices of them, for it cannot eat them in its own mouth solid like its mother eats them for its mouth is very small. So the child only drinks the juices of the food to grow with in its mother's body. Also, that beer the mother drinks, the child drinks a little of it. Hence Azande say about it thus, 'that child who is born with a clean skin, its mother drank much beer.'

When a woman is with child a great amount of blood collects in her body and the child is in the midst of this blood, a little thing like a young rat [or mouse]. It is just a tiny thing surrounded by a pool of blood and it begins to change its form and to grow in this blood. When it has reached the stage of a human being, the blood, in the fullness of which the child has taken its shape, now forms a small net in the centre of which the child lives. It continues to grow in this net. Copious blood collects together and forms the child and its residue makes a net around it. It is this which they call *rikikpwo* [placenta] and of which one will hear it said that such and such a woman has given birth to a child but that the placenta has not fallen. The child remains in this little net [sack] and nibbles at it with its lips and rubs it with its nose until the mother groans, 'hm! hm!' [In pain].

When a woman becomes pregnant her husband goes on copulating with her, and that woman who is likely to give birth soon, the semen of her husband goes with her mucus, they meet together and thoroughly mix with one another and then begin to be in the midst of copious blood. So if a wife does not any more get up and sleep on the floor with menses she sleeps without interruption with her husband.

The child develops in the womb and people begin to notice that the wife is pregnant; and the husband also has it in mind, saying to himself 'it would seem that my wife has been for some time pregnant.' The woman's body all reddens from her being in child and the nipples of her breasts blacken, and her umbilicus rises to a point with her being in child.

When the woman goes among others, experienced women who know about pregnancy will say to her fellows 'that woman over there, she is pregnant, for her belly is swollen tight.' So they start to gossip about her, saying 'the wife of that elder is pregnant.' Her husband waits, and when another moon dies and he does not see her sleep any more apart from him on the ground, and then another moon appears and he still does not find her with menses, and many people are saying that they have seen that man's wife with child, then after three months the husband says that for sure his wife is with child.

He goes to consult the poison oracle, saying 'poison oracle, what I have heard, that my wife is with child, well, that child which is inside my wife, let the oracle confirm that it is my child, of my soul —but no, it is not of my soul, it is of the soul of another man which is in the body of my wife, and while I think it is my child it is really the child of another man—then poison oracle spare the fowl to show me that it is not my child.' The poison oracle looks into the matter and declares that it is the child of the husband of the wife, that it is of his soul, and it seizes the fowl and kills it to the good fortune of the father of the child in that it is his child. Since the poison oracle affirms this he rests in peace with regard to both wife and child. While he waits for the birth he from time to time consults the oracle about the child right up to the time of birth. For it was so for men in the past with regard to begetting, to make sure that the child was theirs and that they were not bringing a bastard into their homes. And men go on consulting the oracle about this right till now.

BIRTH

What is learnt about birth is learnt from hens, in the pelvic region there being a little granulated thing. When people come to prepare a hen for a meal they see inside it where its eggs are; if it is a female bird they say, 'this is the place of the eggs in this fowl, that is where it gives birth to its eggs.' So Azande think that it must be something like that in a woman.

ABOUT GIVING BIRTH

When a woman is in child people get to know of it. Her husband goes to consult the poison oracle. He says to it 'this wife of mine, if it is true that she is pregnant, is it with my child or the child of another?' If the oracle says that it is his child he waits to watch what is going to happen. But if another man has slept with her and given her the child the husband makes a case against him, or he may kill the child. If he does the first, he makes his case before a prince, for the prince to order the man to pay spears. However, if he does not pay the spears quickly the husband mutilates him or kills him.

When a woman is pregnant she avoids these animals: red pig, waterbuck, and eggs; and she may not eat from old pots. However there are some clans which have no such avoidances, like the Angbapio and the Abangbinda—these do not observe any taboos during pregnancy.

When a woman has borne a child she stays indoors for two or maybe three days till the afterbirth has fallen. Then early in the morning they prepare to bring the child out. They go and collect *aumugbe*, *sakperenge* and *ngbege*, and they set light to these woods

in the doorway of the hut in which the child is. After that the midwife takes the child from his mother and comes out with him
through the doorway and holds him over the fire. After that they
collect the branches and light them in the middle of the path to
hold him over the fire there also. However, when they bring the
child out of the hut they cook porridge and manioc leaves. They
then break off some of the porridge and put it on a potsherd; and
the midwife comes to the doorway and calls one of the boys to come
and take it. When he does so they whip him with little switches;
and the boy runs with it to the path and eats it there with his
friends; and after they have eaten it all they smash the potsherd on
the path. The part broken off for the women, they eat what they
want of it and leave the rest. A woman who is about to bear a child
does not eat porridge in the ordinary way but she eats it round the
outside. For if she eats it from the centre in the usual manner her
child's head may become deformed.

When a woman approaches delivery her husband goes to consult
the rubbing-board oracle. If the oracle says she is to leave her hut
to go to another hut, she does so; but if the oracle tells her to give
birth under a tree she also does so. The husband consults the
oracle again about the midwife and who is to sit behind the woman,
and if the oracle agrees to the names put to it the matter is finished
to that point. It is not the business of the pregnant woman to seek
out these affairs of the child; that is her husband's business.

As the child approaches delivery the pregnant woman is in pain.
Her husband sends a messenger to fetch the midwife, the one the
oracle has chosen. Then the midwife comes to arrange everything
for the delivery—together with the other woman who is to support
her from behind. They take the pregnant woman to whatever place
the poison oracle has chosen for her to be delivered in. The husband goes about his work, leaving the midwife with the other
woman helping her. If the pregnant woman's mother is around she
will also be present at her daughter's delivery.

The child sucks the breasts of his mother for a year, or a year and
a half. If the child is often sick the mother avoids the use of old
pots and eats only out of new pots. They name the child when they
see that he has darkened and smiles. It is the father who names the
child; though if his sister is present she may do so. However, it is
generally the fathers who name their children.

A woman who is pregnant does not care to go after other men

but is content to remain with her husband alone. That woman who does not want to become pregnant performs a little act, which is, when she is in her period she wipes some of the menstrual blood on to a little piece of old bark cloth, and she takes this to a distant place where she hides it in a burrow, and she addresses the blood, saying 'you are blood. Do not let me give birth again until such time as I shall bring you out again.'[1] Such is the manner in which she addresses it.

If the child is the fruit of adultery they slay it. They mutilate that man who begat a child by the wife of another, or they kill him.

The kinsmen of the father rejoice greatly where the father is. It is the father who will have possession of the bride-spears of his daughters.

It is the mother of the child who constantly washes him, and she looks after the needs of the child more than does the father. When small children are at home they just do nothing. Some go to set traps, or they play games, or they carry their younger brothers and sisters, until they are old enough to cultivate and take part in hunting. The mother of the child is alone responsible for feeding him. Even though there are other wives of the father they do not give him food.

HABITS OF MIDWIVES

She says 'while I have done work for your child why have you given me nothing? If I had not gone to so much trouble over the child he would have died.' The child's father says 'o my blood-sister,[2] let my child remain alive.' The child's mother says 'o my mistress, let me keep my child; we go with his father to care for him.' The child's father says to the midwife 'just you stay quiet; we will go home to do something nice for you.'

They return home and there the child's mother grinds flour in the morning and catches a fowl to put beside it, and she takes also a spearhead. The father and mother then go to the midwife, they go on till they arrive at her home. The father wants to humble himself before the midwife: 'mother, my mistress, I have lost all

1. A typical example of Zande magical spells.
2. A polite mode of address on analogy to 'blood-brother'. There is no such actual relationship.

my children; you take these things and save my child.' She replies 'it is not for me to say; if you had delayed I would have done the child ill and he would have died, but since you have come right away your child will recover, he will not die any more.' The midwife pays herself a compliment [is pleased with herself]. And she gathers the *Amadi* bulb[1] to cook it in oil for the child. She puts it on the fire. Then she calls the father, 'come sir, with your child.' She takes the child from its mother. She says 'o my grandchild, what is it you are sick from?' She scrapes some of the bulb cooked in oil and puts it into the child's mouth with her little finger. Then she draws cold water into her mouth and blows it over the baby. The father takes a spear and places it on the ground, saying, 'o mother, you instruct us well about the child.' She says to the mother, 'you eat this bulb for your child in your breast-milk.' Then she collects all her things, for it is finished. She says 'o mother, sleep at home a few days and then bring the baby for me to see.' The mother replies 'true, my mistress, I shall not stay away for long; one day soon I shall come to see you.' She and her husband then leave for home. This brings the business of a midwife to an end. There are bad midwives, those who want to give bad sickness to newborn infants. This sickness, of the kind called sickness of the *Amadi*, is that which kills infants, or almost kills them.

BABIES' FOOD

Among Zande foods they refuse to tiny children is porridge—they do not give porridge to babies—they refuse it to a baby, and also dried beans. When a child has reached the stage of taking solids, when they are eating meat they do not give him any with bone, and the same with fish, such as the fish, *aguru*, which are very bony. They keep all bones away from a small child. They also keep away from him the vegetable, *nomba*, saying that it would smell in the child's body. Also that sorghum, which is *bozagbora*, would be too powerful a food for a child to eat—it swells up a child, so they may keep sorghum away from a child. Also the yam, *manzi*, because they say it irritates a child's throat unless it is cooked till it is sodden and soft and they can put it in the child's mouth. Also beans,

---

1. A magical plant called after the neighbouring Amadi people, who are supposed to have first used it to protect newborn babies.

because they might twist a child's inside. Also salt, for if a baby eats salt, the salt will boil over in his chest and the child might die. So they keep also salt very much away from babies. And the leaves of manioc also, they do not give manioc leaves to a baby to eat as it might die from them. Also crabs, Azande do not like to give crabs to their babies because they are hard. Also the oil-bearing gourd, *koforo*. Also roasted things, because a baby does not have the strength to chew roasted things, for one does not grind roasted things. Also caterpillars, they keep all caterpillars away from babies. Babies eat the yam, *gbara*, if it is boiled but not if it is roasted for that would twist its mouth. Also the fruits of the rubber vine, they do not give them to a baby to eat because they would boil over in his chest and he might die. Also things like skin, they would not give skin to a small child to eat for it might choke him. Thus the only food they give to babies to eat is that which will not make them ill, that is what Azande give to babies from among their foods.

A MAN AND HIS NEWBORN BABY

'O child may you not be angry, may you be peaceful. O my child, you who are my only son, all my children have died to leave me with only you two, you and your sister. I am favoured by you. As I have begotten you my child may you not flit away from any unhealthy troubles. So if it is the ghosts of my father and of my other kinsmen—you go away from my child so that he may be perfectly well. I take away the ghosts from the matter. If it is witchcraft which troubles my son I will discover that.'

MARRIAGE

Well, in the past when a man was to marry he went to where the father of the girl was, that is to say, a man who wanted to marry a wife for his son, the son being still a bachelor. If the father was a friend he said to him 'o my friend I have come to marry a wife from you.' The other agreed, saying 'if you have any oracle poison take it and bring it with some chicken and we will consult the oracle about the girl's future. If the oracle gives a favourable prognosis you can marry her.' When he brings the poison they take one chicken and say to the oracle 'this child of mine, if that man marries her, will she long be in his home? Oracle spare the fowl? She will not be there for long, then oracle kill the fowl?' If her future was bright her father said 'since the oracle says you are to marry her, you give me spears.' When he had given all the spears his in-laws were ready to hand her over. They therefore brewed beer, ground flour and caught a fowl to send them with her to her husband's home. Those people who accompanied her to her husband's home, they made presents to all who accompanied her; and they made presents to his mother-in-law; and then they departed, leaving his wife behind. Then man and wife remained for good together, though the wife would visit her father's home on short visits, returning to her husband again, until such time as she bore him a child.

(1) In the past a man engaged himself to a girl by placing a ring or a knife in her hut. When this girl grew up into an adult woman they paid ten spears; and then they paid no more for a very long time. When she was old enough to have a home of her own they paid another ten spears, and then the relatives of the woman at once handed her over to her husband.

(2) In the past if a wife did not bear her husband children her relatives would give another of their daughters to him to bear him children to his spears. However, when they gave him another woman the husband gave a further twenty spears for her. If this second wife did not bear a child the husband said nothing about his spears, because the relatives of the women would say that he was unfertile, since they had given him two women.

(3) In the past if a wife bore only a male child and no female child they did not return the marriage spears. It would be the responsibility of that male child to make a case with his maternal uncles, claiming a girl from them, whose marriage spears he would take.

(4) In the past those matters about which husbands felt badly and for which they drove away their wives were these: adultery, laziness, meanness, witchcraft, ill-will and dirtiness. It was for these things that a husband used to drive away his wife; and it is still just the same today. When a husband drives out his wife the wife's relatives return his spears. However, the wife's father returns the spears minus one, for he keeps one because his daughter had made up the fire of this man and had prepared food for him also.

(5) Those matters about which a woman leaves her husband are that he leaves her alone in her hut, not sleeping with her, and that he is mean with her, and towards her relatives also. These things, when a husband does them to his wife, she does not like it and leaves her husband, and her relatives return his spears to him.

(6) In the past a wife used to leave her husband on account of his impotence, and her kinsmen returned his spears to him. This matter was taken before the prince, and the prince would accept the wife's statement, saying that it were well that the woman should leave her husband as she wished to do.

(7) When a man takes a wife and they have no child they know that it is the wife who is barren when the husband takes another wife and begets by her. Then everybody knows that the wife is barren, because the husband has had a child by a different woman. But if he takes two wives and then does not have a child by the second one they say that it is he who is barren. And if a man takes a single wife and they have no child and then later the woman leaves her husband and takes another husband and this second husband begets by her they declare by that happening that it was the husband who was barren. It is by such means that they know who is barren and who is not.

(8) When they return a woman's bridewealth her father keeps one spear among the bride-spears because his daughter kindled her husband's fire and prepared his food also. However, those things which the husband gave to the mother of the girl, they do not return them at all, they would stay with her for good.

(9) When they return a husband's bridewealth, all those things he gave his in-laws out of charity, he does not keep a record of those things, they are all free gifts.

(10) A big prince marries a wife just as Azande do, except that a prince hands over the whole twenty spears at once to the girl's relatives and she at once comes to the prince.

(11) In the past a Zande would marry the daughter of a great prince with forty spears and she went to her new home at once.

(12) In the past when a man's wife died in his home he collected a fee and took it to her kinsmen, and they gave him another wife in the place of the one who had died. If they did not give him another woman they returned only ten spears and kept the other ten for themselves since the wife had died in his home. [Only if she had given birth to a son.]

(13) If a mother died leaving a son and the relatives of the dead mother held on to the child, not letting him go to his father, this child, when he has grown up, would make a case against his maternal uncles because they had kept him without reason on top of his father's bride-spears. The prince would accept the son's plea.

(14) If a man's wife dies at her parental home her relatives return his spears. If they have no spears they give him another woman to take the place of the one who died.

(15) If a woman dies of witchcraft at her husband's home and they consult the poison oracle and it reveals the witch, then the prince says that the witch is to pay a penalty to the dead woman's kin since he had killed their child without reason. The husband has nothing to do with this payment of spears.

(16) If a man marries a wife and she dies of witchcraft at her parents' home, and they discover the witch responsible, they take him (to) before the prince. The prince tells the witch to pay twenty spears to the dead woman's relatives. Then the woman's relatives give that man whose wife has died another woman; and they take their share, which are the spears.

(17) In the past if a widow refused to take a husband from among her husband's kinsmen then her relatives would return the spears to the dead man's kin. Then the widow would look for a new husband on her own account, of a different clan, and marry him.

(18) If a widow says that she will not take her husband's younger brother but will marry a more distant relative, such as the son of his elder brother or his sister's son, the people pay heed to her decision and consider the matter very carefully. But if the widow sticks to her decision then her relatives consent finally. But although they consent the younger brother of her husband feels bad about it, for they are the real kinsmen of the man. [Later the younger brother would make a case or leave it to his son to demand a wife from the new husband.]

(19) If a widow says that she wants to marry an elder brother of her husband and his younger brothers say it is no matter, he is like our father, let him take a wife for his younger brother and take the widow for himself. So they leave her for that elder brother of theirs. He will consider their interest by himself.

(20) If a widow says that she wants to marry a son of her husband and if her husband's younger brothers make a case about it before the prince, the prince himself sends for the widow to question her,

and if she sticks to her determination to marry her husband's son the prince agrees, and there is no more talk about it.

(21) If a child dies, his maternal uncles pay ten spears for the mother's pregnancy-belt[1] to his kinsmen or to his father also.

(22) If a man begets a daughter and she is married; and after this the father disperses all the marriage spears to his sons and then dies; then if the girl leaves her husband they have to return all the spears to him.

MARRIAGE OF AN ELDER

How does an elder get a wife? An elder in the course of his journeys sees a nice young girl at the home of an elderly neighbour and he begins to make a special friend of this elderly neighbour. They get on splendidly. Then one day he prepares himself carefully, and shaves off his beard clean. Then he takes some five spears and sets out to go to his friend. He continues on his way and arrives. His playmate[2] gives him a stool and he seats himself. They begin to exchange badinage and then, when they are silent, he says 'my friend, I have not just come on a visit; I said to myself that I would come to ask you about that young girl I have seen here. I said to myself that since all elders are alike[3] you might be charitable to me and let me marry her and become your son-in-law, my friend. Alas so! She herself may say that she will not marry an old man, for that is their habit, they like only young men.' A girl who pays attention to her father, when he summons her comes at once and seats herself near her father. He says to her 'o my child, you have seen this honourable elder, how he comes to visit me almost daily. He is now just like one of my kinsmen, if some misfortune overtook me today it is he who would hear of it even before my kinsmen. It would be nice if he could be my in-law, since it is he who would aid me were any ill to befall me. Oh! My child, he is your husband. Oh! My child, do not refuse. However, you speak your mind about it also.' She says 'hm, sir, if he says that he has come to marry me I would not refuse, for you are my father and I would not refuse

1. A leather belt worn by pregnant women.
2. A person who habitually jokes with him. He may be a blood-brother, but not necessarily so. Whether so or not, he is an intimate friend.
3. All, that is to say, like to marry young girls but find age an impediment, especially since European occupation of their country.

what you say, whatever you say, I accept it.' The elder then rises and wipes the ground in front of his father-in-law.[1] When they have taken his five spears he departs.

There are some elders whose wives it is who arrange marriages for them. The wife of such a one sees a nice girl in some place and she asks her, saying 'child, lady, who is your husband?' The girl says 'I am not married to anyone, mistress.' She says 'o child, lady, you come and see me tomorrow and we will have a chat in my home.' The girl says 'very well mistress, I will come tomorrow evening.' Then they separate. The day breaks and then when the sun is sinking this girl comes as she had been told to do. The husband asks his wife 'that girl, where has she come from?' His wife says to him 'sir, she is the wife of a person and has come to visit me.' He says 'whose wife is she?' Then his wife gets angry with [teases] him and says why does he ask her, does he know all the men in the world? She then prepares porridge and gives it to her husband, and she gives hers to the visiting girl also. When her husband has finished eating the porridge she goes to him where he is sitting by his fire and she says to him in a whisper 'since you say that you are not collecting [marriage]-spears any more, you look at that girl who is free and has no husband.' He replies to her 'oh! My wife, a girl like that one, you go and ask her fathers about her. Oh! You marry me a wife thus!' She gets up by his side and goes to the side of her own fire where this girl is. They sit for some time. Then his wife takes a brand from the fire and kindles a fire for him in a hut. She then says to the girl 'mistress goes to sleep in that hut over there, lady.' The girl replies 'mistress, what if he gets angry with me?' She says 'if he is angry you will discover that when you get there.' She goes after this elder [the husband]. She sleeps there. At daybreak the mistress of the home puts water on the fire, and when it is nice and hot she places it before her husband. Then she puts that of the girl on the fire and when it is hot she places it before her. They wash themselves, and then she makes porridge. She places his before her husband, and then hers before the girl. She eats all the porridge and when she has finished she says she will depart. The wife of the elder says to her 'oh! Child, I will certainly come tomorrow to your home.' She agrees and she departs. At daybreak the elder takes his spears, perhaps two spears, and gives them to his wife, telling her to go to that elder and say to him 'o my

1. The Zande way of expressing thanks to a superior.

mother's son, you speak the whole truth to me about that girl I
have seen in your home, for I would like to marry her.' His wife
goes on her way and arrives there to find them [the inmates of the
home] still asleep indoors. She speaks aloud outside. When the
wife of the elder is about to come outside she sees her and comes
outside and greets her and gives her a stool, on which she sits.
Then she goes into the hut and takes up two firebrands and brings
them and places them before her. Then she brings out those of her
husband and makes up his fire. When it has caught well she goes
and brings out his stool and puts it by the fire. He comes outside
and seats himself by the side of his fire and greets this woman, and
she greets him back. He calls for his tobacco and his wife puts it
into his pipe and brings it to him. He puffs away at it for a time
and then leaves off smoking. A little while after he has had his
smoke this woman rises and moves with her stool to near his fire
and she says to him 'master, that elder who sent me with his
[marriage] spears said oh! he has seen an unmarried girl here in
your home; if you are agreeable to her marrying a man you might
find him acceptable and take these ten spears[1] of his while he is
seeking others to add to them.' He is silent and then says 'all right
mistress, but since a person is concerned with her own affairs I am
going to summon her.' He calls her; she comes and sits down
beside him. He says to her 'an elder has sent his spears, saying that
he wants to marry you. So I said to myself that I would ask you to
say what you think on the matter. If it were just for me to say, you
would marry him, for elders make good husbands when they marry
the women of others, better than young men do. Young men are
triflers, they pay no attention to the obligations of in-laws, whereas
an elder does.' She replies 'hm, sir, as he is a man, should I not
marry him?' The wife of the elder thanks him effusively. The
father of the girl takes the spears and puts them away. Then she
rises to go back to her husband. Her husband asks her 'did they
refuse my spears?' She answers 'no sir, he took your spears and
said that they will stay there while you collect others to add to
them.' He says 'good, I am going to seek for spears to add to them
to get my girl to my home. Oh! My wife, if I marry that girl I shall
indeed praise you for her.' Then he goes to collect the rest of the
spears to take them to his father-in-law. Then after some two days
they send his wife to him.

1. 'Two' are mentioned earlier in the text. It could be two or ten.

Husbands and Wives

BRIDEWEALTH

Now, in the past people used to give spears for a wife together with ceremonial knives, billhooks, and axes also; and they gave armlets also; and they gave bark cloth also to the girl's father. They might give nineteen spears and a very large stretch of bark cloth together with them. Bridewealth was also in axes and billhooks and armlets. But today people prefer axes and hoes, and a blanket instead of bark cloth which they used to sew in the past.

DIVORCE

If a wife has relations often with other men her husband divorces her. Also if she does not do her work satisfactorily her husband chases her away; and if she is mean her husband says that she is a bad wife. A woman wants to be released from her husband if he is aggressive and beats her often, and if he is mean with his wife. Then the wife leaves him and runs away to her home. Such a man is a bad husband.

MARRIAGE AND DIVORCE

When a man goes to marry a woman he goes to her father to ask him for his daughter. If the girl's father accepts him, and also her mother, he collects a few spears, some ten, and takes them after his wife. If the in-laws are good people they then let him have his wife on account of these ten spears. But some want to have their full bridewealth of twenty spears before they let the wife join her husband. If he begets a child by this wife he goes on paying spears from time to time to her kin. When his wife dies, or the husband dies, then the union is broken off at once. If a wife leaves her husband and goes back to her kin the husband asks about his spears of her kin. But if the husband has begotten by his wife and she leaves him and returns to her home he does not ask for his spears, because the spears are equivalent to the child. The matter ends there altogether.

Old Times

MARRIAGE

When a man wants to marry a wife he gives a spear to his mother, or if he has no mother then to his sister, saying 'I have seen my wife over there, you go and ask for her hand on my behalf.' She takes the spear and goes and arrives there where this girl is. Her mother tells her to go and place the spear before the father, which she does, saying 'sir, I have come to marry your daughter to my son. My son has asked me to come to marry your daughter and he has sent this spear.' He takes this spear and tells the girl to come because someone has arrived to ask for her hand. She comes before them and her father asks her 'do you wish to marry him?' She replies 'yes father, I want to marry him.'

So they tell her to draw water and heat it on the fire for her husband's mother. She goes and draws water and puts it on the fire and when it is hot she carries it into the hut so that her husband's mother may wash. Her mother-in-law enters the hut, and the girl enters after her; and the mother-in-law washes and then passes the rest of the water to her daughter-in-law, saying to her 'woman, since you are going to take a husband always be clean, always wash well and never again be dirty. Wash regularly so that your husband will always find you neat and clean.' She washes and it is finished, and then she takes oil and hands it to her mother-in-law. Then the mother-in-law says to her 'loosen your hair so that I may dress it, wife of my son.' She loosens it and her mother-in-law dresses it and then gets up to return home and tell her son 'they have given their consent that you should marry the girl my son, so go and visit your in-laws.' The man waits a few days and then he goes to pay a visit to his in-laws, and when he arrives at their place they say to his wife 'go and salute your husband.' The girl goes and salutes her husband. Then they tell her 'you prepare a meal for your husband and place water before him for him to wash with it.' She places water before her husband, and her husband seats himself and says to her 'o my wife draw water for me to drink.' The wife draws water and presents it to her husband to drink, and as he takes the gourd-cup he says to her 'o my wife always wash well so that your body may not be shameful.'

34

Husbands and Wives

When a man starts to marry a wife here, if he is a wealthy man, he gives as his first contribution of bridewealth some five spears, that is, a man who is really wealthy. After a good interval he presents them with another five spears and says [to himself and his relatives] that his father-in-law now has ten. On the strength of these ten spears a man could in the past ask for his wife, and her family would send her to her husband. To begin with she is sent to him for only a short while—she stays with him for only a few days and then her family come to fetch her to take her back to her home.

The husband again waits for some time and then he takes a single spear and goes with it and places it before his in-laws and crouches before them to speak about his wife to them, saying 'o my in-laws do not take my wife from me.' His father-in-law is agreeable and says to him 'all right my son, there is no objection, you shall take your wife. I would not say to you that you must give everything at once now, you might then have to present me with poor spears, husband of my daughter; for bridewealth is like a rubbish heap, a rubbish heap does not cease, a big rubbish heap at the base of a tree lasts for many years, so people say that bridewealth is just like a rubbish heap.'

Then again, after a lapse of time, the season of termites[1] being due, the husband goes to his in-laws and says 'my mother-in-law, I have come to take my wife for termites that she may collect her termites.' Because a woman who has many spears after her in marriage would not think of not collecting her husband's termites, for that has always been the custom.

The custom today is to give spears according to the orders of the European that they are not to exceed twenty spears, and Azande say that they are glad of this because you can pay a great number of spears for a wife, thinking that she will make a good wife, and all she does is to run after men. Then you begin to reflect on the large number of spears you have given for her and that she does this on top of them, and it does not please you. So today Azande say about paying bridewealth that it is not like it used to be in the old days and they are content that it should be so because since the European came women behave very badly. Such is marriage in these

1. One of the main sources of Zande food-supply.

days. So it is bit by bit that they release this girl-wife that she may little by little accustom herself to her husband, for they first send her to her husband's mother. Then, when she gets to know her husband, her father says 'mother of the wife, this woman ought to be sent to her husband for him to set her about his work, for look at his bundle of spears which we have, they continue to increase.' Her mother at once consents but says 'all right, although you must consult the rubbing-board oracle about the day, and should you go to consult the poison oracle you might take a fowl to her name about her husband's place to make sure that if she is sent there she will come to no harm, that the poison oracle gives her a favourable future.' The poison oracle having given a favourable verdict, they grind flour and catch chicken and brew beer, when, that is, it is the big sending-off of her. Her younger sisters carry the flour and her mothers carry the pots of beer, and they all go off together to her husband's home. They arrive and enter his homestead. This husband, had he married wives before, they would begin to prepare a fine meal for this his mother-in-law and to sweep her hut very clean and put the meal before her there. The husband of her daughter then rises and takes a spear and places it on the ground at the entrance to the hut so that his mother-in-law may enter it to go and see her hut, for she would not before have entered a hut in his home, this his mother-in-law. They then take this beer and if the husband is a youngish man and if plenty of beer has been brought they carry it to their father because if the father is alive and there is plenty of beer it would not be proper for them to drink it all in the husband's own home to which they have brought his wife. So they begin to carry this beer to his father's home and his father drinks it and eats the best of porridge and a fowl, and then he blesses [spits on] his son, saying 'my son you have honoured me; you will live long when I have gone.' Such is the affair of taking wives.

MARRIAGE TO BOYS

This is about how men married boys when Gbudwe was lord of his domains. In those days, if a man had relations with the wife of another the husband killed him or he cut off his hands and his genitals. So for that reason a man used to marry a boy to have orgasm between his thighs, which quieted his desire for a woman. If this boy was a good wife to his husband five spears might be paid for him, and for another as many as ten might be paid. A husband who was liberal to his in-laws, they would later give him a woman, saying that good for a boy, how much better for a woman; so if he married a girl his in-laws would greatly profit, so they gave him a wife [girl]. This his boy, he did not abide seeing another near him; they would quarrel and if they took the matter before Gbudwe, Gbudwe told the one who went after the other's boy to pay him spears [in compensation] since he had gone after the other's boy. Also, there were some men who, although they had [female] wives, still married boys. When war broke out they took their boys with them, but they did not take them to the place of fighting; the boys remained behind in the camp, for they were like women; and they collected firewood for their husbands and plucked *nzawa* leaves [for the toilet] and they cooked meals for when their husbands returned from the fighting. They did for their husbands everything a wife does for her husband. They drew water and presented it before their husbands on their knees and they took food and brought it to them, and the husbands washed their hands and ate this meal and then recounted to their boy-wives what had happened in the fighting.

A MATRIMONIAL PROBLEM

This text, taken down from Kamunga wili Nunga, now I am told dead, forty years ago, tells us much about the difficulties a young Zande husband may have with a reluctant wife.

For the first few months of our marriage she acted well towards me. She hoed her small garden, spoke to me respectfully and liked to play and flirt with me. Then her attitude changed; she no longer went about her work and when I tried to play with her she showed herself cold. In many small ways I could tell that she had taken to herself a lover; for amongst us who are Azande in our country a husband knows by many small signs that he has lost the affection of his wife, and that another has gained it. When I used to call her she remained silent in her hut and gave me no reply. When I ordered her to bring me something she used to bring it to me slowly and reluctantly. She refused to lie with me and for three months she avoided my bed and slept on the ground. Whenever I asked her why she treated me in this manner she made no reply but remained silent. I sent for her brother to make my case before him and I asked him to speak to his sister and to tell her to say what wrong I had done her that she neglected me thus. To her brother also she remained silent.

I did not beat her. I remained silent and made no reply when she treated me thus, for we Azande do not beat a new wife. We wait and wait and wait to see how she will turn out. If she proves to be lazy or a woman of nasty habits or a woman who sulks when her husband reprimands her, then we send for her brother who is her lord because he is the owner of the spears with which we married his sister. We make our case before him and we tell him that we did not just take his sister from him but we gave him spears in compensation. We married her legally—well! What ails the woman? In what way have we wronged her? Let her speak it to her brother that we may hear it! Well I spake thus to her brother and when I found that she continued to treat me in this improper manner I spoke to her father and mother about it also and told them that I wanted to know why she thus refused the bed of her husband. But to her parents also she kept silence.

Well, I did nothing, I let her be. I was dutiful to my parents-in-law and paid them frequent visits. On these visits I often found Mafata in their homestead. I held my peace and watched him while he built a hut for my mother-in-law. Himself, he built the mud walls, by himself he cut the uprights of the roof and bound them together with withies, by himself he thatched the hut every part of it, and completed the hut. I spoke to my mother-in-law and said to her 'my mother, what affair is this? Why do I always see this man Mafata in your homestead? I come to see you early in the morning and he is here. Why has he built you a hut? He is no relative of yours.' My mother-in-law replied that he had sponsored her son in the circumcision rites and that this was the reason why he had come to build her a hut. I said 'what an affair is thus, mother. If it is the custom for a man to build a hut for the boy whom he has tutored in the circumcision rites, well, I have never seen it done before. The boy will come and build a hut for his sponsor, who is his elder, this I have seen, but never yet have I seen a man build a hut for his pupil, who is his younger.'

For we Azande in our homes here do not act thus, as the old men will tell you and the princes also. For many Azande cheat in this way, for a race of cheats are the Azande, they carry on love affairs with the wives of their neighbours under the cloak of 'sponsor' or 'blood-brother'. The mother of the girl who is deceiving her husband, if she is a bad woman, will connive at the deception, and her father also. They will take spears from the lover secretly in the bush in payment for their daughter's services. They will call upon him to build them huts, to bury their dead and to perform all the services which are encumbent upon a real son-in-law. If the husband of their daughter asks them 'why is it that this man acts towards you as a son-in-law?', they will reply 'you talk as a child, is he not my blood-brother, is he not my son's sponsor, does he not act so in virtue of the bond of blood?' But in replying thus they deceive, for men have love affairs with the wives of their neighbours under the guise of blood-brother and sponsor. When we Azande hear that we say 'it is probably a lie.' It is thus.

I remained silent and made no reply to their explanation. I waited. Some time later the government called upon the men of the government settlement in which my father-in-law resided to leave their homes and go into camp for ten days into the bush to build a bridge over the Yubo, that bridge over which one crosses when one goes to the country of Ngere. So my wife said that she was going to visit her father at his work on the bridge and as I said nothing she went. I slept two nights and then I said to myself, 'my father has gone to do ten days government labour, it is well that I go to see him and to sympathize with him and say "oh my father, you do indeed labour!" ' So I went and as I arrived, I saw the little grass huts which the men had built to sleep under during the period of work. I asked, 'where is the little hut of my father-in-law?' They told me and I went to greet him. He said to me, 'you have come my son?' I answered, 'yes, my father, I have come to see you at your labour, truly you are working hard!' I said to my mother-in-law, 'mother, you are indeed present?' and she answered that she was indeed present. I said, 'what matter is troubling you?' and she answered that there was nothing troubling her. I asked her, 'are you at peace?' and she said that she was at peace. Well, my father-in-law was very pleased with me for coming to visit him at his work. He

said, 'my child, you have done well to come and see me. It is
good thus.'

Then I looked round and saw my wife in the door of her
father's grass hut. I greeted her there, but instead of acknow-
ledging my greeting she turned around and entered the hut. I
said to my mother-in-law, 'my mother, what affair is this? What
wrong have I done your child that she treats me thus?' She asked
her daughter, 'what is troubling you that you act in this way?'
Her daughter replied from the hut, 'if I had a knife, I would stab
him with it.' Her father said, 'no, no! Child, why do you speak
thus?' But she remained silent.

Well, then I looked about me and I noticed that the owner
of the grass hut next to that of my father-in-law was Mafata.
So I said, 'this Mafata, this sister's son of Tupoi, what does
he do here?' My mother-in-law replied that it was indeed as I
had spoken and that she did not know why he had built his
grass hut next to theirs, for it was not right that it should be so.
I said, 'o, my mother-in-law, this Mafata built you a hut in
the past and always I used to see him in your homestead, now
when you have all left home to come and stay near your work, I
find that he has built his hut next to yours. What affair is this
mother? Oh, mother of chiefs, if he is a secret lover of my wife,
you speak it!' My mother-in-law replied, 'If it is thus I have no
knowledge of such an affair. Should I consent to his secret love
if I know of it? Is not Mafata a son of the clan of the Abangombi?
How should I have any such dealings with the children of the
Abangombi? Was it not a child of the Abangombi who in the
past blew his magic whistle against me and tapped me on my
arms and legs with it so that I was sick almost to death?' When
my mother-in-law spake thus, I was silent. For amongst us who
are Azande, a man does not argue with his mother-in-law for
there is shyness between them. A man must honour his mother-in-
law. It is not customary for us to answer a mother-in-law when
she speaks in this vein. One says, 'yes, mistress, it is indeed true
as you have spoken it,' and then one keeps one's own counsel.

That night I slept in my father-in-law's hut and at daybreak,
as he was going to work, I said to him, 'my father, I came to see
you at your work, now, I will return home with my wife.' He
consented saying, 'very well, my son, you have done well to come
and visit me, return home together with your wife.' He saluted

me saying, 'you are indeed about to depart?' and I returned his salutation, 'yes, father. I am about to return; you will remain?' He replied, 'yes, son, I will remain here with my work.' So he departed to hunt for stones to make the bridge. Seeing which I called to my wife that we should depart and return home together for she had slept three nights with her father and mother and it were well that man and wife should return home together. She remained silent and did not come out of the hut. So I departed with the little son of my father-in-law.

Now amongst us who are Azande, in our country here, when a man takes a wife he will choose one of her small brothers and will treat him very kindly and will be generous with him, giving him often plenty porridge and rich flavourings and perhaps also making him a present of a knife. The Azande act thus so that the child will come and tell them any secret intrigue afoot between his sister and another man. For a child sees these affairs and his big sister will say to him that what he has seen must remain secret and that on no account must he disclose her love affair to her husband. But the child will just acknowledge her words and will then wait until he has seen the whole of the affair so that he may report it all to his sister's husband who has been kind and generous to him. This is a Zande custom.

I departed in the company of my little brother-in-law, and we walked together homewards. After a while I said to him on the path, 'oh, son of my father-in-law, you act well towards me and tell me about this affair which is between my wife and Mafata. Listen well to my words, my younger brother, and tell it all to me, oh my mother's child.' He replied, 'your wife is deceiving you, for she has made a secret love-bond with Mafata. Always it was he who plaited her hair. Throughout the day he was working on the bridge and at night your wife crept secretly into his hut to lie with him.' I said, 'child, you speak the truth.'

We returned home together and I waited and waited. Towards sunset my wife came along the path by herself. I said to her, 'what is the matter with you? Is it not proper for a man and his wife to return home together?' She did not reply but entered into her hut. I said nothing, but remained silent to see what she would do.

Well, she refused to lie with me. She declined to wear the cloth which I had bought for her from the Greek at the Government fort, but wore just leaves instead, which she had plucked in the bush. Now, a man likes to see his wife with nice clothes around her loins, he is happy when he sees her thus and her body well oiled and her hair freshly plaited, for when she is thus he wishes to play with her. But my wife refused all my advances. She wore leaves instead of cloth around her loins, she covered her body with ashes and rubbed them on her arms and head and face as she sat by the fire, whereas, when she was with Mafata she was always well clothed and oiled. Now, when a woman acts in this manner she does so because she does not wish to appear attractive in the eyes of her husband, so that he may not desire her. But her husband knows that she is acting deceitfully in order to commit adultery with another man.

I did nothing till my mother-in-law came home when I remonstrated with her daughter and asked her, 'what wrong have I done you that you treat me in this way? If I have ill-treated you tell me so that your mother may hear the ill that I have done you. If I have taken to myself a love, you speak her name so that your mother may hear it.' But she remained silent.

Later she took up a fine glass bottle that I had bought for her and in which she kept her oil for oiling her body, and she threw it out of the hut against a tree and smashed it. Her mother said to me, 'do not answer her, but collect the pieces that I may go with them to show them to her father.'

Well, I was tired of this affair because she was always in a bad temper with me and was ever sulking in her hut. Some days she would not cook at all so I went hungry. She became lazier and lazier; she did not hoe her garden; she did not make a maize-bed around the huts; she did not clean my homestead; rather she used to sulk all day in her hut and scrape away the walls and eat the mud which she scraped from them. She refused to lie with me but slept on the ground in her temper. Well, we Azande think that it is good for a man to beat his wife. All men beat their wives because if a wife has erred and you beat her, she will understand that she has erred and will remember her error and not fall into it again. But a man will not beat his wife without good cause, only a fool would do that. For women are in truth like children who need correction. It is thus in the eyes of all of us who are Azande.

However, I said to myself, I will not beat her yet for it is not well to beat a new wife. Rather, I will wait and see what is going to happen in the future. I thought much on the matter, and I came to this conclusion, that that man Mafata, the sister's son of Tupoi, had shut her ears so that she no longer heard my words and that he had come to ruin my home with his deceptions. For when a woman takes a lover she wishes always to lie with him and not with her husband. Her lover will try and persuade her always to act in an ill-tempered way towards her husband and always to disobey him so that tiring of her company he may rid himself of her and then she will be able to marry her lover. For it is thus that women act amongst us Azande, for they are sly folk. In my opinion it was so the land lay.

So I went to see Bage [a prince's deputy] to make a case before him. I told him that in the past my wife was pleasant in my eyes, but that now she was spoiling the peace of my home with her ways since she listened not to the words of her husband, but to the words of Mafata, her lover. I told him how Mafata had built a hut for my mother-in-law, and that a man does not build a hut for the mother of the boy he has sponsored in the circumcision rites, amongst us who are Azande. I told him that Mafata had built this hut for the mother of his lover and that he had done so under the name of sponsor. Bage replied, 'it is true what you have said.' Then I told him how my wife had followed Mafata to the place where they were engaged on government labour, and that she had followed after him under the cloak of going to visit her father, and how when she was there she had gone in after him into his hut after dusk. When Bage heard this he sent a messenger after the child who had told me about this affair, the child of my father-in-law, to ask him whether it was true what he had told me or whether he had spoken out of spite or malice. The child said that it was quite true, and the messenger brought back his words to Bage. Bage replied that indeed enough had been said and that I should take the case to Gangura [a prince].

Then I went away to the house of my elder brother and I there took a little fowl and went into the bush to consult *benge* [the poison oracle] about this affair. I said to *benge*, '*benge*, if indeed it is true that Mafata has copulated with my wife, not simply spoken with her or made advances to her but has actually lain beside her, then you kill this little fowl, twist it in spasms and throw it to the ground. If he lay with her before I married her you are not to pay any attention to that. Do not kill the little fowl on that account, but if he has lain by her side since I gave spears [bridewealth] to her father, then kill the little fowl. If this is untrue, Mafata has not copulated with my wife, and her little brother spoke falsely, *benge* you spare the little hen, let it survive.' *Benge* killed the hen about him. Later, on a second occasion, I again consulted *benge* and again *benge* killed the hen to the name of Mafata. So I took the hen's wing on a stick and I went to show it to Gangura. I spoke my case before him and I laid the wing at his feet in order that he might see that I had not come to slander Mafata, but that I had consulted *benge* and that *benge* had consented to my suit. Gangura told someone to call Mafata. Now, I had already spoken to Mafata and had said to him, 'speak the truth to the prince so that he may hear it and this affair may be finished.' Consequently, when he came before the prince he spoke without fear and said that indeed in the past he had made a love-bond with my wife before I married her, but that he had given up his affair with her since a long time ago. Gangura asked him, 'when you were her lover had anyone given spears to her father?' He replied that Pilipili had given spears to marry her at the time when he made a love-bond with her. Pilipili had paid spears to marry my wife with them, but he lay with his mother-in-law, that is, with the wife of his mother-in-law's brother, and this is a very bad thing to do amongst the Azande, for in our eyes it shames a man's mother-in-law. In the past they would not even have given him back his spears, but now that the Europeans have come, people no longer do as they did in the time when [King] Gbudwe was alive. Pilipili was the man who did this shameful thing to his mother-in-law, so they returned his spears to him and they accepted mine instead.

When Gangura heard that this Mafata had been the lover of my wife, when she was the wife of Pilipili, he was very angry and said to him, 'man! You! Why did you go after the wife of another man to become her lover? You go and make your speech in the outer court, do not come here to speak it before my face.' He told him to give a test to one of the old men about the court that he might know whether it was true, as he had spoken, that he had not gone after the daughter of Bamina since she had become my wife.

Gangura then asked the daughter of Bamina if it were true that Mafata had been her lover and that he had left off the intrigue. She said that it was just as Mafata had spoken it. Then I rose and said to Gangura, 'oh prince, my lord, for four months my wife has lain on the ground and has refused my bed, and if it is indeed true that she has not had intercourse with Mafata then surely there is another lover. By the limb of Gbudwe, by your head, she is deceiving me, for I asked her why she refused my bed and she was silent; her father asked her and her mother also what wrong I had done her that she refused to lie with me on account of it, but she deigned no reply. She gave no reason for her behaviour. Oh prince, I have done her no wrong, why therefore, should she trouble me thus unless there is some man behind her who speaks ill of me to her and turns her against me. It is as I have spoken, my lord.'

Now the prince saw that my case was good, for in the eyes of a prince it is not well that a woman should refuse her husband's bed, for a man marries a woman because he wishes children. When he feels desire for a woman he calls his wife to his bed and it is an evil thing if she refuses him. If, on the other hand, she is in her menstrual periods, she will act quite rightly in refusing him; but the prince will know that a dishonest woman will often refuse to have intercourse with her husband, making the excuse that she is in her menstrual periods. But if she is an honest woman she will show her husband the blood on her thighs so that he will know that she is speaking the truth. For women are great deceivers. It is an ill business when a woman acts thus for then her husband goes after the wives of other men and brings trouble on himself. Moreover, it is not well in the eyes of the prince that a woman should refuse her husband's embraces without cause. A man plants maize in his maize-bed and he expects to eat of the maize. The thing is a thing of shame, so the prince thus speaks of it in the form of a proverb.

Now Gangura saw that I had a good case so he told my wife to select one of those around her to give him a test to consult *benge* about her case, and he said let the test be in the eyes of *benge* whether Mafata had lain with my wife or, if not Mafata, then some man had gone in to lie with her. Well, Mafata gave his test to one old man of the court and my wife gave hers to Bodoli, the personal servant of Gangura. *Benge* spared the hens to their names [found them innocent] but they consulted *benge* dishonestly. For when I consulted *benge* the hens died and when they consulted *benge* the hens survived, so that it looks as though they possessed the *benge*-antidote, *zigabenge*, which they used to corrupt the oracle. For if they wished to consult the oracles fairly why did they not do so in an honest manner. You see their game: Mafata gave his test to his relative-in-law, the husband of his father's sister. An honest man does not give a test to his relative-in-law. My wife gave her test to Bodoli to consult *benge* with it but he passed it on to Gangura's deputy Nagu. This is not correct procedure, never before have I heard of a man instructed to consult *benge* passing on the instruction to another. So I told Gangura all about it and he said, 'that is true,' and turning to one of his deputies, Banvuru, he said to him, 'listen, you consult *benge* about his case.'

As it was new moon, Banvuru did not at once consult *benge*, but he waited until the moon should have risen high in the heavens. Meanwhile, my wife had been sick, so I waited until she had completely recovered, then I went to lie down beside her. Oh, it is a thing of shame to speak about! She pushed me away from her; I seized her arm; a struggle ensued; her brother came with a cane in his hand and struck me with it. My brother-in-law's wife also came to pacify us and she was struck. They said that I struck her, but I did not strike her, for it is wrong to strike one's mother-in-law. However, I made her a present to compensate her for the blow. Then I followed after my wife to my father-in-law's hut in the bush, for he was sick and was living in a little grass hut in the bush, as sick men do.

I stated my case before my father-in-law and he approved of it. He asked his daughter what wrong I had done her and she was silent. So he said to me, 'your case is good. You have spoken the truth; I do not at all want to return your spears. But if again there is any disagreement between you and your wife do not beat her but come and make your case before me and I will settle it.' I replied, 'you have indeed spoken truly, my father, you have spoken well, master, you have settled the case fairly. I have paid attention to your words, master, and in future I will do as you say.' So I wiped the ground in front of my father-in-law [in thanks] and said to him, 'I came to speak my case before you, now I will return home.' He acknowledged my farewell greeting, saying, 'yes, my son, you return home. Your wife will sleep here tonight and then she will follow after you. Meanwhile, I will admonish her.' I departed and went home.

After two days, my wife returned to me, but her heart was sore against me and she would not speak a word to me. I waited, and after a few days, I went to a dance. I danced and beat the drum and then returned home. When I arrived in my homestead, I looked everywhere, but I could see my wife nowhere. This was a very bad affair in my eyes.

MEALS

That elder who has several sons does not often eat with his sons. He sends meals out to them to his outer reception hut, the older ones. He eats his meals with his little children, those who are just small, because he is an elder. He who has only one wife, if he has only one wife and they are just man and wife together he wants always to eat meals with his wife together. Such a man who does this, of him the better-bred people say in their talk [quarrelling] to each other 'am I like you who eats meals by yourself and with your wife and are therefore not a man used to the court; so that you speak such nonsense about me.' So Azande speak about the matter with regard to such people, such a one as his fellows do not often eat at his home: 'friend, that man eats with whom?'

Some people say 'you are stupid if you just eat meals with your wife alone.' It is this that men dislike, those who are well-bred, saying that they would not eat from the same dish just with a wife, for one of their friends might turn up, a true man of the court, and he might see him eating alone with his wife, then could they ask him to come and sit down and partake of the meal since they were eating with a wife alone.

So those men who are well-bred arrange to eat separately from their wives by the fire, for it is shameful to eat together. An elder likes to be angry with his son, saying 'child, a son of mine should not eat often with his mother lest he grow up in the habit, for were he to grow up in the habit that son would not become a strong man like me.' So elders speak about it to their sons, that they should

47

separate in the matter of food from their mothers. When they go for a meal, the children of an elder, his male children, all go to where their father is, they go to seat themselves there to eat a meal—so it is that those who beget sons admonish them about it, for such is the custom about eating.

A WIFE PUTS FOOD AWAY FOR HER HUSBAND

The Azande are the sort of people who do not abide hunger in any circumstances. When the season of cultivation comes they cultivate their gardens well, for if they did not cultivate their gardens well they would have no food at all to eat. Such an elder as is well-off so that many people come to his home to hoe his cultivations, and he gives them a meal and beer, will not eat like those who suffer from lack of food. His wife cooks a meal and she breaks off his portion and she hides it in a hut; and she gives the rest to him and the people with him. The other portion she hides in a hut; they call it 'the something kept to eat' for when his wife reserves it for him he does not know before that there is any food. If he knows the habit of that wife who always keeps back some food for him in a hut, then if his wife gives a meal to him and other people he will not eat much of it, for he knows the habit of his wife and thinks that she has hidden away his meal for him in a hut.

A MAN'S ADMONISHMENT TO HIS WIFE

Now, a man marries his wife and he says to her 'since we are going to marry, well, about what you will have to do, when my relatives come you will have to cook meals for them for if they come as guests you cannot refuse them, for when people are on a journey they do not take food with them. Someone will give a meal to a travelling guest. If you do not give hospitality to your relatives then when you go to their homes they won't give you hospitality. If you give hospitality to my kinsmen, my people, it will be well; and if I make any mistakes with regard to your relatives, that I must be responsible for. Also, don't make difficulties about my wives and say that you don't want me to take another wife, for if you get sick who is going to prepare meals for me, who is going to draw water for me, and who is going to bring me firewood, and who is going to gather leaves for me? For I am a man. A woman does not marry a man just to talk, a woman marries a man by her hand, that is, for work and to prepare meals for her husband.

'Do not shame me, if you shame me I will shame you too. If I do you ill you tell my kinsmen about it that they may hear of it, for I am a loyal servant of the prince. You prepare food for me to eat with my friends—that is what makes a happy home. And I don't want you to have intercourse with other men; that will be your death, because if I see you with other men I won't ignore it and I won't leave the man alone either but I will kill him, for I wearied myself in seeking spears to marry you with them.' So a man speaks to impose order on his home.

'And that matter of placing warm water before the husband daily and grinding *kurukpu* stain for him to anoint himself with it—and you must wash my feet for I am your husband, for that is what I married you for. And when you cook meat don't scrape the top off it. And when I kill my animal don't cook any of the meat for a lover; just cook it for me and my friends to eat. This admonishment I have just spoken to you, if you do what I tell you I shall be pleased with you. If I do you ill you complain to my kinsmen. And that business of shaming me in the eyes of men, that is insulting me. . . . And another thing, no stealing, no taking the things of another in your hand. Another thing, do not insult anyone when you are on the path, and if anyone insults you, you let our prince know of it and he will summon him, and if the case goes against him he will have to pay you compensation.

'And with regard to the wife I shall marry after you, don't refuse her use of your mortar, don't refuse her use of your winnowing-basket, don't refuse her use of your grindstone for her eleusine; for if you were to do these things it would show malice. If you are pleasant with my other wives and have a happy relationship with them in the home, then when I marry wives I shall honour you in that they share the home with you in peace.

'There is a wife who goes fishing and catches a really big fish and cooks it for you out of regard for you—then I will summon you to have some of it—or it may be rats or the food with which they escort a new wife of mine, you shall eat of it, you must not reject it for that would show malice. When my mother-in-law comes you must prepare a meal for her—that is the mother of your friend [co-wife] with whom you share the home—that shows a friendly home.

'If I give you spears to go and marry me a wife with them do not delay with them on the path, because if a woman delays on the path, one whose husband has told her to go with spears after a wife, then he will not have his spears accepted, or if they accept them then they will later return them.

'Another thing: do not spoil my food. It is for you to give it to me. Another thing: you must not be difficult with me on account of your bananas, and when you see your bananas are ripe pluck them and eat them. Whatever it is you prepare do not hide it for yourself, do not put it away for yourself. When you catch fish come and show them to me. An honest woman, when she catches fish brings them home and shows them to her husband before drying them because a wife who catches fish and does not let her husband see them is a mean woman and a thief, or maybe she has a lover for whose sake she hides this thing from her husband to give it to him. And when you go away make sure that your fowls are looked after because a man might need a fowl to consult the poison oracle with it at a moment's notice should anything untoward happen.

'And also I must not come back from a journey to find that the fire has been allowed to go out. It were good that when I returned I should find you at home. Much better stay at home and look after the gourds on the rubbish heap and plant the sweet potatoes and the manioc and the groundnuts and the nettle beans and the earth-peas and the maize and the ground-yams and the climbing-yams and your sweet sorghum; and plant your bananas.

'I admonish you much, for a relative may come to your home to die of hunger there.' The wife says 'all right, I understand that you speak at length. Since I married you, you have admonished me much about habits, but if I am the sort of person who listens to advice I have taken in what you said to me. Only God can make a person go straight and if God makes me do the right thing with you you will not have to blame me; for since I came to make a home with you you have not deceived me. And if you are thinking of women, all right go ahead and take another wife, it will not upset me. It is only bad if you get women deceitfully—only if you take lovers would I make trouble with them and complain to the princes. I would not give anything of yours to a lover—I would not give oil to a man to anoint himself with it. I would not give your stain [*kurukpu*] for a man to anoint himself with it. If you gave me seeds I would not eat them—for if a husband gives seeds to his wife she must keep them to plant them in due season so that when they fruit he may sell them for spears and also give her her share to cook and eat. What upsets me is that you marry a woman. . . . Truly you say that you are a prince's subject. You give me a hoe and leave me to cultivate with it while you go off. What about cutting down the trees for me so that I may get on with the hoeing. And this talk about women! I don't mind how many wives you marry—so much the better for me, for we will rest peaceably with them in the home, and when they cook meals I shall partake of them, and if I am sick they will draw water for me and look for firewood also. And that business of hiding things—do not do that—if you want to give something to another wife, well, give it to her openly, for to hide it from one to give it to another is just about saying that one is a witch and that is why the gift is made secretly; and I don't want malice in the home; my mother was a wife among many.

'Those things you do not like, which you object to, tell them to your kin and whatever they say is wrong in my conduct let them correct it and I will give it up. So just tell me what it is and I will give it up right away. And another thing, If I upset your relatives in any way just tell me what it is and I will give it up. And if I catch a big fish I will not conceal it from you—you will see it, that fish, before I dry it. And I would not sit around in a person's home for long as though I was awaiting a meal, just leaving my hoe at home. For you men are very ready to accuse a person of wantonness, and if you accuse me of wantonness, saying that I gave something of yours to a man I shall insist on proof of that, for I would not think of taking a man's thing—people won't shame me by saying that a certain person's wife is a thief. And my mother was not a tale-teller, and I am not a tale-teller; for you men are like water in a bowl,[1] and if a person does not understand that, he will be in trouble with you. And that is true, for if a man sees his wife with another man he wants to use a weapon against him—just for nothing, as it were dew which dries on your foot. So is the favour of a man. And I would not, if I saw a man's bird in a snare, take it, for if I did so and cooked it for you it might be that the owner

1. This expression here has the sense of 'impulsive'.

has made magic and you would die, and then people would say
that I killed you and then it would be a debt for your relatives and
they would have to pay my kinsmen compensation for saying that
I killed you. My mother did not give birth to wild cats. You may
say that I hide things from you, but I have hidden nothing from
you, for mother wearied herself with looking after father, and
when I live with a man I make sure he has plenty to eat; and also
I make sure that you receive first-fruits to eat, for you might hurt
yourself on a stub. And that business of my giving you first-fruits
of my plants and you return them to me—then our things will
flourish and people will want to buy them from us, bringing
spears to buy our things from us. However, it is not a man's duty
to take care of seeds, that is a woman's job; for as I am here, that
which you dislike, you tell me of it, for if I eat seeds, well, you
tell my relatives who will make it bad for me, saying that it is not
up to a man to take care of seeds, and if his wife eats them it is
shameful for her, for it is a thing of shame. Also I don't know
how to cook just a little food, I cook big flavourings, right to
the brim of the pot, and however much the husband eats there will
be some to put aside for him when he feels hungry again. And
when you give me things don't take them away to sell them or
you won't see wrinkles on my face. And don't give any of my things
to another woman secretly, for that will not please me and I might
have to make a case about it before the princes and elders. And
that business of meanness you speak of—well—if I catch fish by
all means come and inspect them, there is no harm in that. And if
I am lazy you tell it to my kinsmen and they will correct me. What
upsets me most about you is that when I cut grass [for thatching] it
is just left to rot and you don't build me a hut. If you were to
build me a hut and weave me a door and get me some mats and
generally make my home pleasant, then if you get around, it will
not matter. I won't speak ill of that. . . . And also build me a
granary, for I want to put my pots in my granary. . . . And if
I find a good grindstone you must go with me to lift it to my
head, for if it rains I shall stay inside your hut to grind my thing,
and another woman might hide her grindstone from me. You
carve me a mortar. I will gather my clay and you find a friend
who knows how to make pots and tell him to mould the clay, and
when a pot is made you can give it to me for my flavourings.
And if you find a bowl you can buy it for me and then I can eat

my food from it; also a stool, you get me a stool; also a knife; and also an axe for making my salt. Also you can beat out bark cloth for me to wear. Well, we have talked a lot and what we have said—if anyone says anything just out of spite we shall know it, because many are the little ways of us women and there are some who are spiteful while others speak truthfully, for women are timorous about errors. . . . But I leave off, I have talked much to you.'

BARRENNESS

Some men are infertile, and also some women are barren. A man marries a wife and is with her a long time and she does not bear him children. His younger brother marries and begets a child, leaving him where he was; and his yet younger brothers all beget children, and he not at all. He goes to consult the oracles: 'this affair which has troubled me, is it due to women?' The poison oracle says to him 'no'. He asks again: 'and my father and my mother, is it due to them?' The oracle says to him 'no'. 'Those old sisters of my father who come to my home, is it they who are responsible for my trouble?' 'No'. Then an elderly in-law says to him 'ai, my son-in-law, how are you going to unravel this affair? It was not thus with me as with you. Have you consulted the oracles about your mother-in-law? I am giving you the hint because your father was a good friend to me, was your father.' He replies 'I went to see my elder kinsmen to ask them to consult the oracles about my mothers-in-law, but a fowl did not die to them. When I went into the matter with my father's elder brother the oracle said nothing at all to indicate them.' His in-law covers himself up with talk: 'o my child, since, when I tell you something, you say I am talking rubbish, whom will you listen to?'

The older man uses up all his chicken about his own affairs. When the younger man thought that he was going to consult the oracle the other began to consult it about his own affairs with the rest of the chicken: 'child, loosen one little fowl so that I may discover the condition of my cultivations with it. Leave that little brown one and take that little black one that I may enquire about the condition of your mother with it.'

WOMEN'S WORK AND MEN'S WORK

Now, a woman's work in the home is to make and keep up the ridge of earth and sweepings round the courtyard, to hoe the cultivations, to weed the eleusine, to plant pumpkins, to weed the oil-bearing gourds, and to draw water for her husband, and to cook the meals [a wife who cares much for her husband will, if there are many guests, break off some of the porridge with its flavouring in case her husband has not eaten his fill so that when he enters his hut she can give it to him in the hut]. A wife also digs up groundnuts and brews beer and threshes eleusine and winnows the eleusine grain, and she gathers firewood and she grinds the eleusine and she cuts grass for thatching huts and she builds up the fire at which her husband sits; and when her husband goes to collect termites and leaves them to the wife she prepares them for eating; and she breaks up pot clay to be moulded for her uses. She also makes salt by evaporation, catches fish by bailing out water, digs out rats, digs up yams, plants sweet potatoes, strips off the heads of maize, and plucks leaves of *nzawa* for her husband to dry his face with them after washing it in the early morning. She also soaks manioc; and she places water before her husband for him to wash himself: and she plaits hair. And she has intercourse with her husband and when she copulates with him she wipes his organ afterwards. Such are her many duties.

Now, a man's duties are to build huts, to fashion [mould] granaries, to carve hoe-handles, to smelt iron-ore, to beat out hoes, to carve axe-handles, to hoe the cultivations, to chop down trees in the cultivations, to weave baskets, to carve mortars, to weave doors; also to hoe virgin woodland [for planting maize], to carve wooden bowls, to make pots for culinary purposes, to plant manioc, to beat out metal thumb-cutters for reaping eleusine, to reap eleusine, to weave flat open-wove baskets (colanders), to weave hats, to weave mats, to plant fig-trees [for bark cloth], to plant bananas, to make bark cloth [by pounding], to carve spear-shafts, to weave hunting nets, to hunt animals, to prepare the hunting area (*gbaria*), to hunt animals by fire, to hunt duilkers, to set snares, to weave fish-traps, to hunt reed-rats, to consult the poison oracle, to consult the termites oracle, to weave shields, to carve gongs. And a man makes a new path, and he weaves filters, and he crushes termites [for oil], and he treads down the path to water for the women. Men catch the *ali* termites and the *awaya* termites and the *ababu* termites. Men catch fish with conical basket traps, weave grass-scoops [for catching termites]; and in the season of the *asua* termites men go to beat them out for their wives and cut pins to pierce leaves with them to catch the *asua* termites. A man constructs the bed in a hut. If there is need to climb a tree it is the man who climbs it, and he perforates gourds, and he spins maize-cord, and he weaves grass for thatching, and he thatches huts, and he weaves rat-traps, and he lays snares, and he copulates with his wife, and he cuts teeth, and he circumcises boys. It is men, not women, who make use of all medicines. Such are men's tasks. They carve wooden bowls, and they construct bridges. All this is men's work.

Now, when a man and his wife make a home what a wife complains of is that her husband does not hoe the cultivations for her, that he does not build her a home, and that he does not provide her with the things a home requires so that she is miserable in his home. Also that he does not have intercourse with her and she sleeps by herself, and she tells him 'I married you to bear children by you'; and she goes and makes a case before his father, telling him that his son does not look after her, and he cannot say that she has done any bad thing: 'since you married me to your son I have not seen any work he has done for me.'

His father summons him to admonish him, saying to him 'the woman's case is a good one, about your not working for her. If you go on being obstinate about it and she leaves you don't blame me, for though I married you a wife it was not for me to build her a hut in your home or to hoe your cultivations for you. You give up your laziness towards your wife and go and dig up clay to build a hut with it for your wife. You just roam around and do not stay at home; you just roam about, and if you have intercourse with somebody's wife I am not going to pay compensation for you, for I married you a wife.' If he is one who listens to admonishment he says that what his father has said is true; and when his father has departed he goes and takes an axe and goes and builds a hut for his wife and builds her a granary also and in general makes a decent home for her and hoes a fine cultivation to go with it, so that there is no more a disagreement between them.

And a wife might go and complain to the prince about all her husband's faults, and when the prince has heard her case he says 'she speaks correctly. When a man marries a wife he must work for her, build her a hut and do such duties in the home as are his, for well has his father admonished him about them. If when people give you advice you don't take it and you treat women in this way you won't have any wives. You build your wife two huts, for she needs one for guests, for if guests come they can sleep in one while you sleep in the other; that is why a man builds two huts in his home.' Then he tells the wife to go home with her husband and if he does not do his work she can make a case.

And another thing: a man buys seeds and gives them to his wife to plant at the season of planting, and he sees no more of them. Then the man goes to his wife's father; early in the morning he appears and tells her father that he has come to complain before him about his daughter, so let her come to answer. Then the wife comes and sits and her mother also comes and sits, and the husband says 'since I married this wife of mine she has not done any work, she has just been idle. When I bought seeds for her and gave them to her I have seen nothing for them in their season. Let them ask her. Her father questions her, saying 'you have heard what has been said, is it true?' She replies 'what he has said is a lie. He bought just a few seeds and mice have eaten them all up, and so he says it is I who have eaten them. And with regard to what he says about my work, what he says is lies.' Her father questions her husband again 'does she not hoe in your cultivations?' Her husband replies 'no. While she just wanders about, grass sprouts all around her hut. And since it is like that I just lack a wife. I might just as well not have one, for when I am hungry I have to go and eat at my mother's home. I am tired of the whole business, and I am sick of trying to get a meal. After all, a man marries a wife to be looked after by her.'

Her father's wives interrupt with 'what the husband says may be true.' When all have had their say the father of the wife says 'now, what you complain about this man, that he has not provided you with a hoe, that he has not bought you seeds, and that he has not set you up with the proper utensils of a home—well, he says for his part that you are lazy, and there he has a good case. He has done you no ill. . . . However she will not return with you today

—her flour must be ground first. Early tomorrow morning you can return home with that silly girl.'

So at sunrise next morning they collect together their things and go off with them—and with their flour, and she and her husband depart. After they have returned home the husband goes again to his wife's father and tells him that they decided in his favour, that she stop being lazy. Her father says 'all right, the case went in your favour.' Then if she persists in her laziness her husband says that he gives her up since her father has admonished her in vain; so let them give back his marriage-spears, let her return to her father and let him have his spears back. Her father says that he has given away the spears, but let the husband wait a while and he will find some more for him. But the husband says to him that since he told him that his daughter was a stupid no-good why did he give away the marriage-spears; it might be that he wanted him to go and make a case before the princes. If they don't give him back his spears he takes the matter to the prince and says to the prince 'I married the daughter of so-and-so and I paid him marriage-spears and then when his daughter proved to be stupid and lazy I complained to him and he admonished her in vain; so since she persisted in her ways I said that they must return my spears. I put the matter before you, that he has not returned them.' So the prince sends a messenger to summon him; and when he arrives the man who is making the case stands forth and says to the prince 'that man has my spears. I gave up his daughter on account of her laziness, so I say let them return my spears which I gave them.' The father of the wife then stands forth and says to the prince 'I am not going to make a fuss about this. I told him that he had right on his side in that he could not be expected to put up with her laziness. I have no more to say; I have come to hear what you have to say.' The prince asks the father of the girl whether he has said that he has given away the spears and he replies that he has given them away. So the prince says 'since you have used his spears to marry a wife—well, he has given up your daughter on account of her stupidity, so you must return his spears to him, because your daughter is stupid and lazy on the top of his spears. But since you have nothing to return you must give him the wife you married with his spears.' If he is very fond of this wife he marries her younger sister and brings her to the court and says to the prince 'o master, since one does not take away a man's wife from the hut I have married her younger sister in the path of the spears and I have brought this girl with me.' The prince says 'all right. She is a woman—you take your wife and give the other to him to marry with your spears.' The husband agrees. Then the messenger says that he wants a gift from the husband before he can go off with his wife. They must pay him his fee, before they can take their wife, for the trouble he has had in arranging things. When that has been done they may take the wife home. Such are the affairs of husbands and wives.

WHAT WIVES DISLIKE

Those who are wives—a husband a woman has married weaves a hunting net and goes and kills a beast in it and takes it and keeps it for himself in its entirety. Then his wife collects 'the dung of the net' [the bark of the tree from the bast of which the net was woven, here meaning the entrails of the animal] and throws them into the bush [to spoil his hunting]. He takes the wife's pot and says to her 'bring the pot here.' He cuts off some meat and puts it in the pot, then he cuts off another piece and puts it in the pot, and then a third piece; and he looks at the meat, the three pieces, and he says 'woman go and cook this my meat.' The wife cooks this meat and cooks porridge and she takes the undivided meal and gives it to him. He eats the meat till he has finished it. His wife watches him, watches him and keeps silence.

He kills another animal and the same thing happens as before. The wife goes to visit her friends and sits among her many friends. One of them says to her 'eh my sister, does your husband look after you well?' She replies 'yu! O my sister! That man, that man, he is not a human being, he behaves just like a dog. My sister I am miserable with that man. He is not a man, he is just a nasty fellow. My sister, the cord of the net, I threw it away [to prevent him killing more game]—he goes and kills a beast and keeps it entirely for himself. If it were you sister you would not count pieces of meat. He counts his meat saying "one, two, three", so he counts them for me to cook them for him.' The other woman replies to her friend 'my sister, that kind of man, I would not marry such a one.' The first woman goes on to say 'I stay with him for the sake of my father; if it were just a matter of my mother I would have left him. But it would seem that my father has spent all his marriage-spears [the woman's bridewealth]; so I am miserable thus; he has no spears to return them.

'I cooked his meal, washing my hands very clean, and I served it to him, and he went and said I had eaten some of his meat. I was angry inside myself, thinking that alas I was most unhappy here with my husband. Then one day he went hunting again. An animal started to run in the bush and came and saw his net, left his net alone and came and caught itself in the net of another. So he took down his net and came home with it and appeared in our home here and took it and threw it to the ground; and he said to me "a beast came today and stood before my net and just looked at it and nothing more, and then it ran away to die in the net of another." '

A wife hears such words from her husband and she just says 'hm', otherwise she keeps silent. He also keeps silence and goes away to consult the rubbing-board oracle. He consults it about various people in vain; then it sticks to his wife. He returns home and says to her 'my wife I have been to consult the rubbing-board about my net and the oracle says it is you. Therefore you blow out water so that an animal may soon die.' She answers him *'uwo!* Who? I? When you killed an animal did you see its teeth in my mouth? *Ye o!* O women! When you killed it you shared it all round with everybody, but you did not give me, your wife, even the entrails, the entrails of the net. All right, you kill your beast and I go and pluck manioc leaves in the bush to cook and eat them. It does not seem possible that you, my husband, should kill a beast and that I who married you should eat nice things at your hand. I am for you just a little slave. Do you not know that I am mistress of the net. I would just be troubling my mouth to blow water on your net; do I eat the animals? What a mean man are you!' [The man speaks] 'all right, if you act like that [if you don't want to give me meat] we will just eat manioc leaves. If I go again to the bush, by my father's loins I shall hurt myself on a stump of wood on account of my spoilt hunting or a man will spear me in the net because my fate is bad.' She answers him again 'shame upon you; and even if you don't go into the bush it does not matter to me, as when I stay here I don't eat meat anyway.'

Such is the talk that women sit to talk about their husbands; they say that such-and-such a husband, when he kills animals gets out of it altogether and leaves the entire carcases for his wives and it is his wives only who have anything to do with the cooking of the meat, the husband just eating and nothing more; he is a man of pleasant temperament, a man one can respect; but that husband who counts the pieces he gives his wife to cook is not a pleasing character.

WOMAN'S WORK

When a man marries a wife her work is to prepare food, to draw water, to gather firewood, to sweep up the ashes in the huts, and to put warm water before her husband in the early morning for him to wash himself. Her job is also to make beer for her husband. Also she must keep her courtyard clean. And when her husband builds a hut she must cut the grass for thatching.

THE MURDER OF NGBANDIA

The man Ngbandia, his years in the earth are some seven today [he was killed in 1921]. His wife arose, whose name was Nambiro. Her brother came to reside near the home of herself and her husband Ngbandia. He came to reside near them. This lad lived there for a time and then fell sick, and he died. After he had died they consulted the poison oracle about his death. When the oracle had killed a fowl about it they said that the mother of Nambiro should observe the taboos of mourning. They summoned a man called Gimo and told him to come and make medicine, for the oracle had selected his medicine. Then, when the medicine had been made Nambiro considered, and she said to Gimo that she had nothing with which to pay for the medicine. So she said to Gimo that since she had nothing with which to pay for the medicine he had better come and kill Ngbandia, her husband, and then she would be able to marry him, Gimo, as his payment for the medicine, for she had nothing else with which to pay him for it. Gimo said to her that since she spoke about the matter in this way, that man who was constantly threatening Ngbandia about his bridewealth, the man Zelebingba, who had paid it for the mother of Ngbandia, for he had not returned it; it might be well if he [Gimo] went to call him so that together they might slay

Ngbandia; and should he agree they would go about the matter without delay. As soon as he had spoken in this manner to Zilebingba he said that that would be all right, he himself had already been thinking so also. When it was dark he would come and they would go together. When it was dark they came and arrived near Ngbandia's residence and there they waited. Nambiro came and saw them and said to them that they should await a little, for she was preparing a meal for him; then, when he entered his hut for the night, she would call them so that they might do that deed they had come to do. So she cooked porridge and gave it to her husband Ngbandia and he ate it and entered his hut. When he was in his hut he started on his twining of twine for his nets, for he was a great maker of nets. So she left him at it and went and told them to stay where they were for the present, for he was twining his cord and had not yet gone to sleep; when he was asleep she would call them. So when sleep overcame him she took his axe-handle and his short stick with which to beat his cord: and she took these things, and when she had given the axe-handle to Gimo and the short stick to Zilebingba she took for herself a hoe with its handle in her hand. When all was ready they said that they had better make up some story in case somebody asked questions. They told Nambiro that as they were going to kill him, should anyone ask her about her husband she must deceive him by telling him that it was the sons of Dangba who killed him; she must never mention their own names, she must put the blame on those men. Then they went and entered the hut after Ngbandia and the two men struck him together and at the same moment on the nose as one man, even as there were two of them. He tried to cry out but could not do so. Then his wife appeared at his side and she repeatedly hacked at his nose with the hoe she had in her hand, and he died right away. When he was dead they brought him out of the hut and they tied him up into a little bundle. When that was done they began to bury him in the rubbish heap which was at the edge of the courtyard, where they always emptied the ashes. Then they said to the woman that she must wait there till it was light and then thoroughly clean the inside of the hut and the courtyard of his blood. So when it was light she thoroughly swept the place, and she collected the ashes and emptied them on top of him. When that was finished she began to collect her things and she fled to where her mother was, to reside there.

After that, on another morning, another of her brothers, who lived quite near their home, arose in the morning to go and fetch some eleusine seed from his sister, Ngbandia's wife. He went on his way and appeared in the centre of the homestead, and he called out in vain for his sister, for there was no answer from her. He entered the hut and he saw the eleusine seed behind the bed and he took it, and he saw a hoe also and took it as well. However, this hoe was the one with which she had hacked at his nose. As he was about to take it outside he noticed that the hoe was bespattered with blood; and when he examined the eleusine seed he saw blood on it. He thought to himself that they had killed an animal and had gone to hide it in the bush [so that people would not know they had meat]. He walked round the vicinity calling out in vain, never a voice answering him. He then went to summon other of his kinsfolk so that they might go to her mother's home to make inquiries there. So they went on their way and arrived at her mother's home; and when they looked around and saw her they said to her that since they saw her here, where was Ngbandia? She told them that Ngbandia had said to her that first thing in the morning he would go to the east to eat Abari medicines [to obtain magic from that people]. But this did not seem credible to them, so they went to [Prince] Gangura to tell him about it. When Gangura had heard all about it he asked after Kuagbiaru [the narrator of the story], but vainly, for he was not present. Then he summoned that man who was next in seniority to Kuagbiaru, whose name was Dimoango; and when he presented himself Gangura told him to go and see Nambiro and bring her that he might question her about Ngbandia. He went on his way and seized this wife of Ngbandia and brought her, and when he came to where Gangura was Gangura asked her 'where is Ngbandia? What animal did you and Ngbandia kill [and cut up] in the hut?' She tried to speak but could not do so. They then said to her 'you are a cheat [liar].' She said to Gangura 'it was the sons of Dangba who came the other day to kill him, the six of them.' Gangura collected four of his police and told them to go and seize the sons of Dangba and bring them for him to question. They went and seized all the sons of Dangba and brought them to Gangura. However, Kuagbiaru was not present. Gangura asked them, saying to them 'you tell me about Ngbandia, why you killed him.' They replied 'by your limb prince, why should we kill Ngbandia? What feud is there between us and him that we should kill him on account of it? This woman, she is lying about us for no reason, so that the Europeans may kill us. There is no feud between us and Ngbandia.' Gangura said to them 'since you so firmly deny it you had better send a messenger to your father Dangba for him to provide fowls for me to consult the oracle with them to your names. If the fowls die to your names I will hand you over to the Europeans.' Gangura took Zilebingba and the other man Gimo and he sent them after chicken to Dangba's home; while it was just these men who had done the murder, namely Zilebingba and Gimo; Gangura having no idea what had happened. His mind was made up that it was the sons of Dangba who had killed him. As they were on their way after the chicken Kuagbiaru himself appeared, he who was one of Gangura's leaders of young warriors. When he arrived Gangura was quite unaware that he was in the court. People told Kuagbiaru how the affair had come about. When they had finished he said that they [the sons of Dangba] were to be brought out of the hut so that he could have a look at them and question them also himself. When they brought them out and sat them down I, Kuagbiaru, rose and told them 'right now I want to hear a true account from you, I do not want any lies. For Gangura has said that homicides and any other sort of case should be dealt with by me [by way of a preliminary inquiry]. You sons of Dangba, you sit quietly. If it was you who killed Ngbandia, it is you I will hold.'

I then took my cord and bound her [Nambiro's] feet together with it, and I took both her hands and pulled them between her legs. Then I tied her up all over so closely that no bit of skin showed between the strands; she appeared to be just a little bundle. I then attended to her mother and I tied her hands behind her back, and I tied her legs together with cord as I had bound her daughter. I then took a longish cord and made a reef-knot in it, and I took hold of her lower lip and drew it into this knot, and I tightened it pretty hard. I told her that Ngbandia's death was her affair and if she did not disclose what had happened she would be in trouble right now. As I gave it another tug the flesh of her lip protruded as a little thick bit. She said 'o Nambiro how wicked you are. The death of Ngbandia is your affair, and you just not confess but let me die.' When she had spoken like this and was then silent her daughter, Nambiro, cut in and said to me 'Ngbandia is in the rubbish heap.' I loosened the cord around her and told her

to tell me about it properly or I would tie her up again. I took her
and went with her to behind a hut. I said to her 'I want you to
tell me the whole truth, and if you lie I will straight away tie you to
a tree.' She said 'there is no lie in what I have said, he is in the
rubbish heap in his homestead. But those who killed him, they are
not the sons of Dangba; Zilebingba and Gimo, it is they who killed
him. I summoned that son of Dangba who was Gbanda and I asked
whether he knew these men. He told me that Gangura had sent
them after chicken to Dangba's home and they had gone to seize
them there. I then summoned the kinsmen of Ngbandia and I told
them to go to Ngbandia's home and to search everywhere in the
rubbish heap there. If they did not find his corpse they were to
come through the night to tell me so, that I might go with the
woman herself to search for him. While they were engaged on this
business there Gimo and Zilebingba arrived with the chicken.
I was in the hut questioning the woman. As they came rambling in
people greeted them 'Gimo have you not come?' 'Zilibingba have
you not come?' When I heard this conversation I called Gimo, and
as he entered the hut to join me I seized him, and while I was
binding him Zilebingba leapt up and fled. I tied Gimo up, and
when I had tied him up I started to flog him. When Gangura heard
his cries he sent a boy to inquire who was crying out. Boys came
and told me this, and I told them to tell Gangura that the woman
had divulged about Ngbandia being in the rubbish heap. In the
morning Gangura came into the court and called to me in the hut
to come out of it. He questioned me, and I told him all about the
affair, how it began and what it was about that they killed him. He
said 'o Gimo, did you make your medicine and then go and kill a
man yourself, it not being the medicine which killed him?' Gimo
replied to him 'no, prince.' He [Gangura] told me, Kuagbiaru, to
take charge of them and give them some work to do. While we
were so engaged people arrived with Ngbandia's little finger and
showed it to Gangura. He exclaimed 'Daikada [another of
Gangura's names] oo, so that is how women would kill us and bury
us in a rubbish heap!' It was already quite dark when they brought
in Zilebingba and brought him forward. I took hold of him and
tied him up tightly and flogged him. Gangura sent a messenger to
me and I told him that it was Zilebingba. Very early next morning
Gangura appeared in court. He said to me 'Kuagbiaru, you yourself will take them to the Europeans. Alas, if it had been the old

days, when Gbudwe was alive, I would have speared them with my own spear. However, when you take them you must tell the District Commissioner to kill all three of them; he is not to spare one of them, he must kill them all, including the woman Nambiro, for it was she who began it.' So I went with them and brought them into the government office and handed them over to the Sudanese official, and he put them in prison. However, although they executed the two men they spared the woman. They did not put her to death. So the affair ended.

HUSBAND AND WIFE

When a man marries a wife he wants to see his wife clean, and he does not want her to be lazy in preparing his meals, and he does not want her to go after other men. And if many people come to her home she should prepare nice food for them. Such are the duties a man expects from his wife. A wife wants her husband to sleep with her regularly, to hoe a large cultivation, and to be generous to her kinsfolk. Also for her husband to buy things for her freely. That is what a wife expects of her husband.

A MAN AND HIS WIFE AND HIS WIFE'S FAMILY

A sister sits in her home angry with her husband. Her husband goes after her at night and he says: 'my wife has gone away to come to your home here, my brother-in-law.'
(Her brother): 'yes sir, I did not know before that she had run away. Since it is so, what bad thing does she continue with? Shame to this woman.'
(Her brother's wife): 'my brother-in-law, she is in the hut, you enter a warm place.'
(The husband): '*ai* my lady-in-law, unpleasant is my smell in her mouth this year, lady.'
(Her brother): 'o man, is it true that you have seen men with her?'
(Her brother's wife): 'eh woman are you not in the hut? Your husband is outside.'
(The wife): 'you protect me from your evil-smelling man *ai*!'

(The husband): 'ehe! My lady-in-law do not answer her back, she might shame me right now lady.'

(Her brother): 'friend, go and enter sir. Were you told that the place for your affairs was my home here?'

(The husband): 'you open the door for me lady.'

(The wife): 'ah sir! You are not going to open the door.'

(The husband): 'you there!' (He coughs several times.)

(The wife): 'leave me alone to myself to get some sleep. What is he looking for at night?'

(The husband): 'eh mistress, witchcraft has turned you against me lady.'

(The wife): 'Get away with your talk about witchcraft. Go and sleep on the mat on the bed over there.'

(The husband): 'I am cold. Oh do not things happen! Does a man marry a wife for others!'

(The wife): 'you continue with your bad talk and follow me with it. You will get out right now in the night and return.'

(The husband): 'ah! A man has turned you against me. It is men's talk that you speak to me.'

(The wife): 'ah man! Madness puts you against me oooo! My father! My mother ooo! A man is killing me! My father ooo! My mother ooo! A man is killing me!'

(Her mother): 'eh my son, what are you killing her for?'

(The wife): 'my mother ooo! A man is killing me! Father ooo! My mother the mouth of a man's penis is killing me oooo!'

(Her father): 'oh! Shameless little foreigner, what does she mean by shaming my son-in-law? There is no modesty in that talk.'

(The husband): 'eh my mother-in-law do not enter the hut here after me lady.'

(The mother): 'eh husband to my child you are killing her. Were you told that she hates men, did I not hate men [more than she]? I don't know how I ever came to give birth to her with her father!'

(Her father): 'all of you shut up till tomorrow morning. I will have my say then.'

BURIAL ALIVE OF WIDOWS

In the old days when a great prince died they took one of his wives and broke her ankles and her wrists and they laid her beside the

prince and carefully placed her arm across the prince's body. Then
they began to cover them with earth. Then they took another of
them and slew her on the prince's grave. The rest of them, they
slew them by the prince's fire, there where he always used to sit
with his wives. This is what they used to do in the past in respect
of princes.

PLAINTS

[*Ako* is the most often heard of all Zande interjections or ejacula-
tions, and it is not always easy to find quite the right word in
English by which to translate it, but 'alas!' and 'oh!' will usually
convey the meaning fairly well, though the tone of the exclamation
cannot always be adequately conveyed. In its verbal form it has
usually, if not invariably, the sense of 'to bemoan' or 'to sigh' with
sadness or resignation. When in the translation of the text 'alas'
and 'oh' appear, they are translations of '*ako!*'. And when 'sigh'
and 'bemoan' occur they are translations of the same word used
verbally. Where the words 'plaint' or 'lament' appear they are
translations of the noun-form, *pa ako*.]

Now, the plaint '*ako*' began with want. If a man goes off to
marry a wife and, when he reaches her home, her father says 'you
cannot marry her'; then when this man departs he says 'alas! I
have wearied myself to no purpose, if I had known it was to be like
this I would not have gone there.'

Now, a man rises and goes to visit a prince, and when he arrives
at the prince's home he says to him that he has come to visit him
to obtain from him a gift of spears. The prince acknowledges his
request, and then the man spends some days at court until the day
he is to depart, and then the prince tells him that he has no spears;
and when he is on his way he says 'alas! Have I not wearied myself? Had I known it would be thus I would not have gone there.'
For an '*ako*' is blackening a name. On this man's return home, if
someone asks him 'when you went to that prince, what did he give
you?', he replies 'when I went there he gave me nothing. I have
returned from there with the blackening of a name,[1] which is
"*ako*" on my lips.' The other man asks him 'did you have good

1. It is the prince's name which is blackened, because he was not generous.

meals at his home?' And he replies 'alas, indeed not! If it had not
been for his subjects I would not have survived hunger; they constantly invited me to meals when they saw that the prince was not
giving hospitality. I would not wish to visit him again. Let others
go to his home, because I went to his home and returned only with
an "ako" on my lips.'

If a man goes hunting, arriving at the place of the hunt, stalks
an animal and, when almost up to it, it starts to dash away he says
'alas! That animal, if I had stalked it to get right up to it and had
speared it! It has indeed saved itself. It looks as though witchcraft
spoilt my hunting. Alas! I will go to consult the rubbing-board
oracle.' So after the oracle he goes, and he consults it, and it tells
him that it was witchcraft. So he utters a moan (*ako*) beside the
rubbing-board. Then he goes home and calls the people of his
home and says to them 'the rubbing-board stuck about my
animals. Alas! It is you here who held back my arm in hunting.
Why did you want to spoil my hunting? For if I kill an animal we
all share it together; for meat is good. Alas! What bad people you
are, my wives, what bad people you are; you let a beast die at my
hand so that I go to the bush and return with meat for us to eat,
and then we will not have to moan (*ako*) any more. For what! For
an animal also has ears and it hears things with them. For it is your
witchcraft. I stalked an animal and was close to it when I trod on
some little thing and it leapt up at once at the noise. It looks as
though you trod on the animal's ear against me.' One of his wives
stands on one side and says 'alas! I did not want you not to kill the
beast, if it was my witchcraft you would have killed it.' Since God
gave *ako* together with admonishment (*rugute*) another wife says
'alas! If it is a question of my witchcraft, the animal would have
died. As I know nothing about that thing in the bush it would have
died.' And then she takes water and says 'eh! Where is his spear?
Let me blow water on it.' She takes the spear—he has two wives,
one of them a witch and the other not a witch—and says 'if it is my
witchcraft which is preventing the killing of a beast I blow water
on the spear so that an animal will die and we eat it, for we are sick
of just eating manioc leaves.' 'Alas' is the elder, 'thus' comes after
it. After this woman has spoken her 'alas' about animals she blows
out water, for water is cooling. If a man does not drink water he
will be sighing (*ako*) all the time, for we Azande came through
water to learn all sighs at the beginning of our speech.

So when these women have spoken thus to utter their lament about animals, this man goes out into the bush and when he sees animals he goes to stalk them and he spears one of them strong and hard to the earth, and when it has fallen he stabs it in the neck; and when it is dead this man says to himself 'oh! Did not those women spoil my hunting. Oh! When they had blown water did I not kill a beast right away today?'

This reminds him of water and he says to himself that there is a spring over there and that he would look for it and cut off the animal's tail and take it home with him, so that when he returned he would say to his wives that he had killed an animal. As he was returning home he remembered the idea of '*ako*', saying to himself 'oh! Since I am about to return home, when I get there what shall I say to the wives at home?' *Ako* says to him that he should, when he gets home, just tell them that he has killed an animal. But one of the wives answers 'he!' [in disbelief]. But when she sees the animal's tail she says 'oh! He speaks the truth, its tail is in his hand.' The other wife says 'this is fine.' He says 'oh! Get some baskets and let us go at once for we have to go a very long way.' So they collect baskets and an axe, and then he tells them to put their best feet forward. If one of them is not walking quickly enough he says to her 'oh! You are lagging behind, let us go with all speed, for we have far to go, and if you slacken your pace you will fall well behind us; and we are going to something good.'

Then, when they arrive there they see the dead body of the animal, and one of the wives, she who had caused its death, so that it died, as she goes up to it, yodels, and then she goes to it and strokes its body. She says 'this is a fine affair.' She says 'since it is a very large animal which has died will it not be the death of us?' The other says 'since it is so large and there are so few of us what can be done?' He replies to her 'first get started and in the meanwhile we will think of a plan, but let us first cut up the animal, when that has been done we can then work out the plan I have in mind.' So when they have cut the beast up he says to one of the women 'you take a leg' and he says to the other 'you take a leg, and in the meanwhile I am going over there where there is a little stream so that we can wash our hands in it.'

So they set off and when they get near this stream they put down the meat, and one of the women says 'oh! We must surely go and drink this water which he says he has seen.' So when they reach this water she says 'oh! What delicious water, if only we could make our home near it. The water we drink at home is muddy, this water is really clear. Let us return to this water.' Then, as he has lost his temper with them about his animal, now he loses it again, saying 'who is talking about the home? But you get up and we will go and fetch the rest of the meat; for what we left behind, if a dog is there, it will go after it and eat it all up, go after the animal's leg and eat it all.'

And then when people come the dog becomes savage. It was dog who taught men to steal. As the man is still sulking towards his wives about his home and goes on sulking till they reach the place where he killed the beast there they find a dog starting to eat it. One of his wives says 'it were better if you worked your temper off on the dog.' The dog turns at her and growls at her, and she says to her husband 'alas! the dog is eating up the whole animal.' He says to her 'why don't you drive it away?' She replies 'drive it away with what? It is the dog which has driven me away!' He says to her 'you leave it to me, I am coming.' When he reaches the spot he raises high his spear-shaft and the dog starts off with speed howling at him. He calls to it *sususu* to teach his wives what to do to get out of the way of dangerous animals. He tells them to get out of his way, he would settle the matter in his own way. He cuts out a stick. Since he knows all about angry dogs he silently listens to hear a cry over his animal. He raises his stick on high to strike the dog really hard. As he stalks the dog to strike it with the stick it bites hard on the stick in his hand. But the dog is in pain and flees from the man's meat. Dog says to himself 'they beat me hard near their meat but I will see some way of eating it later today; they won't beat me near the bones. They will eat their meat and then throw the bones behind the bank of earth ringing the homestead and I will eat them, and they would not beat me. However, whenever I see meat all the same I shall not leave it; I shall eat it even if they kill me; if I see a dead beast I shall risk death myself.'

The man says to his wives 'pick up the meat and let us be on our way.' The dog runs and hides, and when the people go away with their meat and arrive home with it the dog follows after them. So while the meat is being prepared the dog waits. The man says that he is dirty and tells his wives to wash him; and then he says that he will go and chop some firewood for a fire for himself to dry himself by it. As there was stubble ready for the fire he goes to break off a stick of wild custard apple to make fire with sticks, and he says 'oh! There is fire in wood!' He says 'fetch some grass to blow the spark on it so that the flame may catch at once and I can break some twigs into it.' The wife puts out the fire, that is, the wind puts it out. She exclaims 'alas oh! The fire has gone out on me.' He answers 'alas! How did you manage to do that? As though my hands were not already abraded enough! Oh! come you and hold the fire-stick firm and I will twirl the upper stick in it again.' They hold it firmly in place for him. He twirls it for a long time and then the friction produces a spark which falls into the stubble. They say to him 'oh oh! It has fallen into the stubble!' He says that he has seen that, and that this time they had better look after it, for if the spark were to go out again he was not going to use the fire-sticks again; they could just eat the animal raw. They say 'alas! How are we going to manage this? We are taking care of the meat and now the fire!' He rises and goes and sits on a log and says to them 'I suppose you think that because I am sitting here I am going to twirl those damned fire-sticks again.' Well, the fire begins to burn all right, and they cut up some of the flesh of the animal to roast it in the fire, saying that roast tit-bits would be nice; saying 'oh! There is nothing nicer than roast meat, how nice is a roast thing.'

Now, he takes the lower part of a leg and roasts it and eats the meat off it and throws the bone away, and the dog then comes and stalks it and runs away with it to well away from the homestead to eat it, sitting where it is; teaching what fear is to people. And then the man begins to erect a platform to place the animal on it to dry the flesh into really fine dried flesh. They say 'oh! Dried flesh is good!'

What they leave raw, flies come and lay their eggs in it, from which hatch horrible maggots. When she sees it, a wife says 'flies have laid their eggs in this meat.' He asks 'what are you going to do about it then?' They reply 'what can we do?' He says to them 'why don't you bind leaves round it? Now, when something is raw you should bind leaves round it, for leaves protect it from flies which might lay their eggs in it. I have been wandering in the bush and seen flies' eggs in putrid animals. Flies are nasty things. You bind leaves round the flesh against them. I have seen decaying animals in the wilderness from which flies arose and in which there were maggots, and I did not take the meat, for a fly goes together with a

dog. Be very much on your guard against both, for they both befoul
a place. As I have gone to the trouble of wandering in the bush to
find my things, that is, my meat, and have brought it back, you
protect it from flies and protect it also from dogs. I don't like eating
blown meat. Oh! You very well know what to do since there is
water, the restorer of things. If a dog seizes food and drops it you
first wash it before eating it; likewise those things on which flies
have settled, you must wash them well before eating them.' He
says 'oh! You must bind it against flies.' But as she has not done so
he makes plaint (*ako*) again, saying 'oh! How stupid of you to leave
the meat exposed so that flies could get at it and people become ill,
maggots breeding in it so that it becomes unclean, for an unclean
thing is one which has millepedes in it. For the fly is gluttonous.
What makes meat edible after flies have been at it is water, for what
fire does is to dry it, with fire it dries, so people say "oh! You prepare a fire at once for that thing, to protect it against flies lest they
blow it." '

So all these matters are matters of plaint. If a woman goes to dig
up sweet potatoes, if one of them is dead she exclaims 'alas! My
sweet potato is dead!' If wind blows down a man's banana tree
he exclaims 'alas! What wind has blown down my banana tree
thus!' If a wind blows down his manioc he exclaims 'alas! How
has my manioc fallen thus!' If locusts eat his eleusine he exclaims
'alas! What an insect has eaten my eleusine thus!' If then he
thinks of the rubbing-board oracle he says 'oh! I am going to
consult the rubbing-board about it.' If [later] the poison oracle says
that a man has bewitched his eleusine and that therefore he will
eat that man's in the place of his own, and if the prince's oracle
confirms this, the prince says that they are to take the witch's
eleusine. The accused man says 'alas! This man is going to eat my
eleusine without cause, for I did not bewitch. A man bewitches in
a dream. However, they say it was me, and they will eat it. Oh!
Since they have sent a war-party to eat it let them have it. Well,
there is something in store for them.' If a man's wife dies he says
'alas! Is not my wife dead!'

In these ways plaints (*pa ako*) began, and they continued on the
lips of Azande as their first talk. So people go about with plaints
(*pa ako*) all the time as the commencement of their talk. So it is
about *ako*, a word which is on all men's lips.

Husbands and Wives

When a man dies his widow goes to live with a kinsman of her husband under the interdiction of mourning. When her mourning has ended she becomes his wife, though if she is old he just lets her live nearby, and he spends much time in cultivating her gardens. She, who is to all intents and purposes his wife, is always nagging him.

If her [new] husband does not make a special effort to look after her she grumbles incessantly. She says 'when my real husband was alive I did not suffer this sort of misery which I now suffer. He did not hesitate to give me anything I wanted from him.' And when she says this she starts to wail and weep about her husband; but she wails to impress her [new] husband so that he will keep her wants in mind. If on some day she goes hungry, then her husband won't get any sleep with her lamentations about her [dead] husband till she falls asleep and ceases them. If her husband does not sleep with her every three or four days she says he is being hostile to her. She talks much at night, saying 'alas! My husband has left me, leaving me in misery. I see people with their husbands and it is like as though I had never been married. I will kill myself after my husband since I am in misery, although the younger brother of my husband is alive and could look after me like my husband used to do.' All these things she says in a wail when regret for her old husband takes hold of her. When they brew beer, if they don't give her a really big bowl of it she abstains from it altogether and will not touch a drop of it. She begins this plaint 'you have not hoed a garden for me at all, you want to let me die from desire for people's things. If you had hoed my garden for me properly it would have been large and I would have been able to make my own beer to drink. However, no matter, you treat me so because I am just a widow who has no further say. You ignore me for your pretty young wives whom you have married; as for me, I am just an old widow.' However, if this man is bad-tempered he begins to say many strong things to her, and he insults her. She rises to enter her hut to wail loudly there. That woman who is resentful will not eat any food they give her, she simply refuses it from their hands. Nevertheless, there are pleasant widows who do not wear out the kinsmen of their husbands, for they always remain quiet and behave with propriety. If the kinsman of such a widow's dead husband does not give her something she says nothing. However, there is something that even she will pester him about, her gardens, that he should help her with them, for she does not want to feel bad about the possessions of others. A widow who acts in this way is pleasing to Azande, for they do not at all like the ones who are always nagging them. Zande wives are great gossipers. If a husband shows that he likes one of his wives more than the others, the others take offence and go and make a case before the prince. Azande are very scared of their wives on that account.

Family, Kin and In-Laws

ORPHANS

An orphan is that child whose father and mother have died, and he has no real kin. He wants to go and live with his father's elder brother. His father's elder brother consents to him in double talk, saying 'Yes my child, now that your father is dead you come and live with us, I shall be delighted. But I don't know; should witchcraft attack you it will not be my fault.' He comes out of his hut in the morning to show the boy where he can live. The orphan then builds his poor little hut and begins his life of misery. He bursts out to the surprise of all 'alas, is not my father dead! I see people with their fathers, *wu wu!*' The elder makes reply 'hm, oh the sons of my kinsmen want me to die!' His wife cuts in with '*hi!* Since the sons of your kinsmen wish your death, do you say that you have any kinsmen?' The orphan hears it and he says '*wowo*, do they not mock me here so!' The wife says 'my husband, did you hear what he said?' The orphan replies 'o woman, my father died and I came to live here to be wearied by you after my father's death.' She replies '*hiiii!* Boy *oo!* I have heard all about you. When your father was alive you behaved in the same way.' Her husband then says 'o mistress, you leave him alone. When I am having words with my son I don't allow that women should butt in. He will see something later on.' When he hears his father saying a lot of things he keeps silent and says not a word more.

HABITS OF ELDERS

Those who were elders in past times did not usually sit much with children, nor with youths. The name of an elder's court was *barasungu* [the place of sitting]—all his children used to sit there. The junior wife kindled a fire for the elder in the courtyard. The youths used to kindle their fire there to sit around it.

The wives of an elder all prepare meals for him; thus if he has five wives each of them cooks for him. Elders do things just like the princes do. These five lots of food, the elder sees them all, and he takes two of them and he places them near himself in his private quarters. And then he calls a boy [to share the food with him]. Then he sends a message to the older boys together with the older sons of his kinsmen who are sitting in their places in his court; the elder sends one of his smaller sons after them. His sons with his followers among them and together with sons of his kinsmen—some ten. The older ones are summoned to the *barondo* [inner court] to the elder himself, some four of the grown-up sons, and they take two of the meals, and they give one of them into the court for the smaller children who are there; and the elder calls the older ones to where he is and they begin to eat porridge with its flavouring; and when the meal is finished they return to the court.

Early next morning they go to whichever wife's cultivation they are hoeing, they take their hoes and go off with them—an elder's hoes would be some fifteen—and all those sons of his, they all go to the cultivations. And the elder himself gets up and goes there as well, to the edge of the cultivations, to direct their work.

Then the wife whose cultivation it is they are hoeing takes two of his wives and sends them back to the homestead to go and prepare a meal for those working for her. If she has any beer she carries it to the cultivations, and when the young men have drunk it they are happy. They cook a meal and take it to them there. They eat it and then go on working till evening; then at sunset they return home.

Those small sons of an elder, they gather firewood and bring it to the court, and they kindle a fire in the sleeping-hut of their elder brothers, and they brush the place clean also. Sometimes there may be three youths in a hut, sometimes two, and there would be two or three boys. They don't sweep the place every day, and they must not cook near the hut; they have to do much work for the elder; and if they do not clean up the place every day the hut becomes very dirty inside. They sleep on leaves, only a grown-up young man who possesses a hide sleeps on a hide.

The youths gather together in the court with their younger brothers and chat. The elder sits in his private quarters with his wives. When the evening meal is finished they all go to him, they

go to where he is and sit with him. They sit around to play; and
the elder gives them good advice to follow.

As for the youths, they are sad in their desire for women. The
elder keeps close watch on his wives to see that they do not go with
the youths. The elder deceives them, saying that he is going to the
prince's court. Off he goes, saying in deceit that he will stay there
three nights. He departs. But he does not sleep there. He sets off
by daylight and after sunset he starts to return home. He rolls up
his sleeping-hide and, stalking noiselessly, he hides in the bush
near his home to await the youths and keep watch on his wives,
and he stays there till midnight. Everybody goes to sleep and they
fall asleep; then the elder comes forth and goes to spy on his wives;
and he opens the doors of their huts in his home and looks around
within. And then he enters and inspects the bed. So he does for
each of their huts. Then he goes to have a look at his young men
and he looks all around their hut. If there is a youth who goes
after one of his wives, if he seizes him with her, he calls out for the
others to come, saying 'look what has happened, that the child
copulates with that woman who is always cooking vegetables for
him.' If it is the son of a younger brother, or maybe his own son,
he drives him away. Other elders say 'this is a bad business'. They
say 'child, you pay your father compensation. Why did you go and
copulate with his wife? Bad is your desire for women since you
dirty your own place!' A younger brother [of the father] says
'leave him to me and let me pay compensation on his behalf. He is
just a stupid boy who cannot go straight.' He collects some four
spears and puts them on the ground, saying 'I am going home with
him. I have shown you some spears and so I will pay his spears.'
If the elder's younger brother pleads with him much they hand
over some ten spears. The younger brother of the elder takes the
elder's son and goes slowly with him to where sits the elder and
with some ten spears with him; and he says to him 'let him go sir,
let him be, he is just a stupid boy who does not know what is right.
Lice eat the head of their owner.[1] That is why I have come with
these spears. Let him be, let him await his death on account of his
stupidity. When he dies they will say that you are his father, you
had to speak in anger to him, that is what killed him.' The elder
replies 'all right. I accept. But let him go and build his hut in your

1. The meaning of this proverb is clear in the context: 'he bites the hand
that feeds him.'

home, he cannot reside here any more, for the women here are much desirous of men and they want to scatter all my sons with their lust for men.'

BLESSING

When a man desires to receive his father's blessing, whenever he goes and kills an animal he presents it to his father first, saying 'my father, this animal, you decide about it; my father, it has nought to do with me, for while you live when I kill a beast it is not for me to decide about it!' He [the father] says to him 'eh my son, what you say pleases me, but if you were like those elder brothers of yours who treat me ill I would not feel so happy.' And when his son is a porter and is paid money for his labour he brings it first to his father. Also he would not eat the first fruits of his cultivations but he gives them to his father. He also goes to make a court case on behalf of his father, his father saying 'o my son, I am too old, you go and speak my case for me.' So he goes to speak his father's case and the case is given in favour of the son's plea, and he takes his father's wife [who has run away] and returns with her and hands her over to his father; and he says to his father 'my father, while I am alive no one is going to tread on you.' His father replies 'o my son! O my son! You shall have my blessing.' His father rises and takes his little [magic] whistle from where he knows it is, being an elder, for he has seen this about his son, and he says to him 'my son! Though I die, this whistle, it will be yours, wherever you go take it with you, do not dispose of it.' So when the son goes before the princes he takes the whistle with him and says 'o whistle! Oh! Did not my father give it to me? Misfortune overtakes me—oh no! My father gave it to me that fortune would be mine.'

CURSING

A man says thus to his son 'o my son you treat me as though you were a stranger; as you have not treated me as a true son it is not well with you. When you killed your first animal you ate it and gave it not to me. You hoed your cultivations, you cultivated your first eleusine and ate it by yourself, and gave none of it to me who am your father. Yes my son, since you treat me in this manner, who do you think begat you?' He says 'yes my son, you have greatly erred. O my son one does not challenge the top of a termite mound.[1] You treat me so, well, after I die you will not prosper.'

He speaks thus to his son and waits for his son to do something really bad to curse him. One day he goes to a beer party at the home of an elder such as Bage, and when they have drunk a good deal of beer the elders begin to talk about their feelings and one of them says to the others 'friends, my sons respect me greatly, any first thing my sons make they give it first to me.' Another then says to him 'o my friend how your sons respect you!' He replies 'yes sir, my sons would not do me ill.' But this man says 'if it were my sons I would not eat of their first fruits; when they kill beasts in their first nets they would not give them to me sir.' Another then says 'what my friend! Your sons have a bad character, mine would not treat me so.' The first says 'sir, my sons do not think of me. Sir, among my sons there is but one who looks after me. That one, when he makes money by porterage, I see nothing of it.' He adds 'sir, look at me, an old man, I will eat no more from my sons. My son might buy me a fowl or set a snare and catch a guinea-fowl for me to eat, but in all these things he treats me ill. Will he get my blessing o! By my limb! By my limb! By my head! By the head of my father! He will be poor till death, and I shall not marry him a wife. By my limb! Snares, if he lays snares for guinea-fowl they will not be ensnared—he will set the snares and see just the image of his father in them. Only let eleusine flourish for him, may just porridge be his portion.'

Another elder says 'sir, if it were my son who treated me thus I would curse him.' The first replies to him 'sir, what I say to you is that he will die in poverty. By my limb here by which I begat him! As I pressed my foot on the bed, as I pressed my foot on the bed when having congress with his mother to beget him, so he turns against me.' When he is by himself he takes his penis in his hand and says 'that son of mine, if he is accused of adultery may he defend himself as an idiot might.' He takes his penis in his hand and says 'this is my penis with which I begat him', and he blows on it. Then the curse pursues him. His son goes and lays his traps, but no animal dies in them. He begins to make something, maybe

1. A well-known Zande proverb, which here has the sense of challenging seniority and authority.

a woven thing like a mat, but he just weaves it to no purpose, for tiredness comes over him as he works at it. When he builds a hut like that of Kisanga the curse takes hold of it. When he threshes his eleusine rain falls on it; and when they start their feast, although he blows his [magic] whistle against rain, rain falls because of the curse. When he goes with others to hunt he kills no beast; he returns empty-handed. He goes to marry a wife to whose marriage her parents have already given their consent but finds that they have since turned against him, telling him that he shall not marry this woman; and they take his spears and return them to him; so he takes his spears and goes home with them, and he just sits by himself in his home and begins to think things over, and he says to himself 'alas so! What is all this?' And then he says 'it must surely be on account of my father's curse which has come to trouble me!' He reflects on what his father might have said in a curse and then says to himself 'oh what shall I do? When I was to marry that woman they took her from me.' He reflects on his father's curse and how he neglected his father in the past. Whenever he goes to speak a case against another at court he leaves the correct course of his plea and talks a lot of nonsense on account of the curse, so that what he says to the prince makes no sense. So people are scared of curses. So people curse their sons; and then a man will consult the poison oracle and ask it 'what my father has said in a curse, is it that which troubles me?' The oracle tells him that this is so. He then says to the oracle 'if I take spears, two spears, three spears, four spears, and go and give them to my father will he bless [spit on] me and pass me between his legs stretched apart so that in the future I may prosper? All will be well with my wives? Then oracle spare the fowl.' So he takes the spears and goes and puts them before his father and says to his father 'o my father, o my father, I will not again do you ill. O my father, you bless me to make clear the way for me.' His father sees the spears on the ground; and what the poison oracle has told him, he reveals it. He reveals it from inside him, saying 'my son, I thought another man was your father, but it seems that after all I am your father. I have not died but am still alive. You indeed treated me badly, so I said I would put you to the test by cursing you that you might do things in vain till you decided to come to me. Yes, I leave off all that now.' Then he says to his son 'sleep tonight and rise in the morning at dawn so that I may bless you to take my hand off you.'

When it is light next morning he comes and blesses his son. So sir this is why people are afraid of a curse.

JOURNEYS AND GHOSTS

When a man goes on a long journey he reaches a certain point and draws water and drinks it and says 'alas! How this path is long, may nothing happen to me on it; may I not suffer injury on it; may a snake not bite me; may lightning not strike me; may I not fall sick on the way. O ghost of my father I am going where there are fangs of snakes, where there are sharp stubs, where there are beasts of prey. O ghost of my father you cut a clear path for me; may not misfortune fall upon me on my way. May no man attack me. O ghost of my father you take care of me on this path, and ghost of my mother also, and those elder brothers of mine who have died. O ghost of my father do you not see me?' Then he blows out water about it *pushiya* and he says 'o ghost of my father may I be tranquil on my way.'

PORTERAGE AND THE GHOSTS

Also with regard to porterage: when a man acts as a porter, that is as a carrier for a European, he goes along until the baggage weighs heavily on him, and then he breaks off a leaf of the *bombili* shrub and says 'o ghost of my father, the baggage is nigh to killing me among strangers, o ghost of my father are you not near me? O ghost of my mother are you not near me? Give me strength to continue strongly. O ghost of my father look how my legs weaken with porterage amid strangers. What shall I do?' He then waves the sprig of *bombili* thus [backwards and forwards] and then strikes his leg with it and afterwards throws it down and continues on his way.

DEATH AND A GIRL CHILD

When the father of a female child dies her elder sister takes charge of her to look after her. Early one morning the relatives gather to go back on what they said about the child. When her grown-up sister comes to fetch her they say to her 'since you have come to take this child away, if anything happens to her there, how will that be? And if later your husband makes her into his wife there is going to be trouble ahead.' Her father's sister speaks out 'o give up your bad habits of the past and rest happily to bring up this younger sister of yours, for you come from the same womb.' She replies 'all right, you decide to speak like that, that if I take the child away something will happen to her in my home, for since she is my mother's child if anything begins to trouble her I should know of it. You are suggesting to me that I am an adulteress, that if I take her away adultery will cause her death.' Her father's elder brother cuts in 'you let her do what she wants; I am not going to give any opinion about it, for the young lady does not listen anyway. You say you have begotten a child; if it were me I would not say that I have a child.' Her husband joins in: 'as you are confusing my wife like this, why are you confusing her in this way? However, no matter, I suppose you are only admonishing her. No misfortune is likely to happen to the child since I shall be around who am a man.' Her father's elder brother goes to consult the poison oracle to ask it about the condition [fate] of this child. If her condition is good he consents to her elder sister taking charge of her. Then they depart for her husband's home.

This child grows up bit by bit and reaches womanhood; and a man comes with his spears to ask for her hand with them. The husband replies 'ai! Sir, it is not for me to consent to a man taking the daughter of my father-in-law in marriage.' However, he says this deceitfully, for he wants to marry her himself. Another man wants to discover whether this man is deceiving. He takes up some five of his spears and comes and appears. He says to the husband 'friend, since you say that no one may marry this girl at your hands, that she is the daughter of your father-in-law, what you say is quite right. However I thought I would come and ask her elder sister. If she says the same then I will go and ask her brothers and they may grant my request. The husband replies 'ai! It seems that things are going to be difficult about her for my brother-in-law does not wish any man to marry her. However, it is her elder sister's business, you ought to ask her. Meanwhile I will go and ask her.' He goes into the hut after her and says to her 'o my wife, since you and I had the responsibility of bringing this child up it would be better for me to marry her. Do not think of consenting to this man taking her in marriage.' She acknowledges the order of her husband and she says to that man 'it does not in any way rest with me, for I am only a woman and could not make a decision in this kind of case. It is my brothers who must decide.' However she is not being open with him for it is indeed her business because it was she who took this girl into her home. This man departs to consider whether to go and ask the brothers of this man's wife about the girl.

The husband of this woman here out-manoeuvres him [to get there before him] with his spears and when he nears the home of his in-laws he first hides his spears in the bush, and then he enters the homestead and waits for a time. Then he breaks into speech, saying to his in-laws thus 'o my in-laws, men are persist-ently asking for the hand of that girl who is in my home and I have told them that since it is not my affair they had better come and ask you about her.' He then waits a long time; and when it is dark he goes into the bush and takes up his spears and he comes and lays them before his in-laws. He says 'o my in-laws, that girl who is in my home, men are intent upon marrying her; but it is I who brought her up, so allow me to marry her as well as her elder sister, so that they may be together. His in-laws say to him 'it is not our affair, go and ask her grandfather about her.' They want to deflect him from themselves because he already has her sister. He goes to the home of her grandfather and tells him all about it. Her grandfather says thus '*ai!* I cannot consent to your taking her after the one you already have in your home, because I want a different man to marry her so that he may work well for me.' However, a man had already brought his spears and given them to her grandfather, and he had hidden them. He then deceives him a second time and says to him 'all right husband of my child, it is the poison oracle which reveals things; if the poison oracle says you are to marry her you can take her in marriage.' However, he cheats him, hoping that he will think that it is his brothers-in-law who refuse him the girl. He says to him 'oh so! You depart and collect the girl and her elder sister and bring them so that we can hear what they themselves have to say.' However, he is just deceiving him.

This man returns to his home and he brews beer, ties up a fowl, and has flour ground to go with it. They come and arrive and he presents all these things to his in-laws. Her grandfather says 'all right, you wait right here and we will go and consult the oracle about your affair.' When he has waited a while they begin to go to the place of the oracle. Her grandfather says that he himself will address the oracle. He begins the consultation by asking about his own quite different affairs, and only when he has finished does he take a very small chicken to ask about the girl. The boy takes it up and puts into its beak so much of the poison that its mouth is full of it, and it dies from this powerful poison, because it is only a tiny chicken. If it does not die quickly he presses it down [throttles it] till it dies. Then the grandfather gets up at once and says that he is going to do some other little work at home. His son-in-law says to him 'but o my master, may we not finish this business first and then you go?' He replies to him 'o my child's husband, where will we find any more chicken? Since that woman [his wife] is difficult about her chickens, what shall we do?' However, he is just cheating him, for he simply does not want him to marry the girl.

He returns home and when he reaches his home he is angry with his daughter [granddaughter] in whose home this girl is living. He is angry and says that she cannot go away with her at all. He is suddenly angry.

Such is the habit of in-laws who nurture the little sisters of their wives. When such a girl grows up the husband of her elder sister wants to marry her as well as his first wife.

MOTHER'S BROTHER—SISTER'S SON

If a sister's son sees a mother's brother with something in his hand he seizes it and runs away with it. If his maternal uncle chases him and catches him he gives him a good beating, and if he is a bad uncle he does not let him keep the thing. But if he is a good uncle he just beats him and he does not take the thing away from him. Sisters' sons take things from all their maternal uncles. Even if an uncle is most distantly related his sister's son seizes things from him.

A GIRL AT HER BROTHER'S HOME

This is about how a girl goes to her brother's home and her brother refuses to let her return to her husband, because he did

not pay him a visit when they were in trouble; and so they keep
his wife until he comes with spears, and then he can depart with
his wife. While she is at her brother's home her brother is anxious
that she may not do anything bad, like adultery, for she is a man's
wife. If she is an honest girl she will listen to the words of her
brother, for they are sound advice. However, a girl who is heed-
less will pay no attention to what her brother tells her; it is to
her ear what the sound of a trumpet is to the ear of a dog, for the
sound of a trumpet means nothing to the ear of a dog. She prac-
tises her deceit and wanders at night after her lovers, and then
she returns home at dawn while her brother is still asleep. If her
brother knows about it he says nothing but waits to trap her. For
he suspects it from the way young men come to visit his home;
he guesses from that that it is they who are practising deceit with
this sister of his. So he waits until she comes to go again to commit
adultery. If he is a hot-tempered man he goes after her to where
she goes. If he sees her with her lover in a hut he stands outside
and says to her 'oh, what sort of girl are you? Why, since you
are a man's wife . . . (rest of text lost).

PARENTS-IN-LAW[1]

'Eh lady you say well, those who are good-hearted, their manners
are the same among men. They are like fire, you eat of it but it is
also dangerous, you sit beside it and guard yourself against it; if
you put your foot into the fire you will be burnt, it will not spare
you. So it is.'

'Yes, that is quite right, I don't want to make things awkward
for him. If things go wrong between him and his wife let him
come and tell me about it frankly and I will settle it. What I
blame him for is that he is a quarrelsome fellow who makes rows,
that is what annoys me.'

'Eh madam, what you say is true. His behaviour is not correct;
if he were a correct person he would not act like that, make a
scene in the home. He would act politely. From what I have

1. This text gives a typical conversation between a man and his wife
about a row their son-in-law has had with his wife, in which the
mother-in-law has got involved. Being a man, he is trying to do the
best he can for his son-in-law while at the same time attempting to
humour his wife who, being a woman, is supporting the daughter.

heard, what I would censure him for in that he has indeed wronged you is that he started to make a row. If he had a grievance he could have told you about it and you could have given your opinion about it, and if it were not correct men used to court would have told you that what you had said was not correct. Men used to court do not hide their opinion from people, they set forth a man's bad case. If a man has done wrong it will be bought to light by the men at court to the people.'

A BOY AND HIS PATERNAL AUNT

'O my brother's child, how are you?'
'Thank you mother.'
'And how is your father?'
'He is very well mother.'
'And what are you and your father eating nowadays?'
'O my father's sister, my father has not killed an animal this season. Alas we and our father are hungry. Father said, my father's sister, that you are to send him food by me; also to give him back his axe for him to cut down the brushwood in his cultivations. Also he said that you were to come to him unless you were sick; but if you are well he would like to see you. He very much wants to see you again, his sick sister who is now well again. My father's wives are making trouble for him. What he said to me, that I repeat to you; and if your husband has some oracle poison perhaps he would ask the oracle about his condition and then I could tell him the oracle's verdict.'
'O you penis! Have you seen any chicken around? You just tell my husband to find us some chicken!'
'My husband, your in-law asks you for oracle poison so that he may find out if he is going to die, for he is very sick and he may not live the season out.'

A MATERNAL UNCLE'S WIFE

[The father says] 'you go away to your maternal uncle. I don't want you around here. I have got quite enough to manage with my little children—we will make our home with them. I just begat you and there were no other children [by your mother] after you. The marriage-spears which I gave to marry your mother, there was no daughter on them. You go and make a case about her and make your maternal uncles give you a woman with whose spears you can marry. Now, when you are in your maternal uncle's home just look around—there are chicken in his home and nets too, and as my material uncles are all dead, you go and if you find a net just take it so we can hunt with it.'

So off he goes to his uncle's home and he greets his uncle's wife 'o wife of my uncle, where has my uncle gone to?'

'Ha! Do you not see that penis that you ask me about?'

'Eh wife of my uncle, I ask you about my uncle.'

'Sir, just stiffen yourself beneath the granary. Your uncle is hoeing in the cultivations.'

'Eh, right you are. O wife of my uncle I am very hungry.'

'Ho! man, you! [more insulting expressions]—is this where you expect to get a meal?'

'Eh wife of my uncle why do you abuse me?'

'Why do you leave your uncle hoeing and come and worry me here?'

'O wife of my uncle you are shameless, does one shame a sister's son?'

A MAN AND THE SON OF HIS ELDER BROTHER

'Oh, son of my elder brother, since your hand came out of the net, since you have grown and are strong, it is from you that I should receive things. Eh child! Why do you treat me so? Did we not beget you?'

KINSHIP

The kinship of a man with his father's elder brother is also true kinship. However, while his father is alive he calls him 'my father's elder brother'; but when his real father is dead his father's elder brother, or maybe his father's younger brother, takes him and brings him up. After that, this child calls this father's elder brother 'my father'. But if his father is not dead he calls him 'my father's elder brother'. With regard to the kin on the father's side, if a man wants to talk to his father's kin he calls them all by their proper names; he does not avoid their names at all.

The kinship of a man with his mother's younger sister is true kinship. When a man talks with her he calls her 'mother', for he avoids the proper names of his mothers; he must never call them by their proper names. And the kinship between a man and his mother's elder sister is true kinship. He calls her 'mother', for he avoids also the proper names of his mother's elder sisters.

A man does not call his grandparents by their proper names, for he greatly respects them; and when he talks to them he addresses them as 'grandparent', for it would be above his station to call them by their proper names. A child would never call his father by his proper name. When he talks to his father he makes himself small before him, calling him 'master' or he may say 'my father'. A child addresses his mother in the same way. A child avoids his mother's name. However, he does not talk with his mother with any embarrassment, for she is his mother; and he does not hide his affairs from his mother at all. But he addresses her as 'my mother'. However, a man addresses his sisters by their proper names, for he does not stand in any respect of them; and if his sister uses bad language to him he gives her a good beating. Boys do not respect their sisters at all while girls are a little afraid of their brothers, for they fear their beatings. A man speaks of his wife's kinsmen as 'my in-laws', but he addresses most of them by their proper names; but is in great fear of the adult ones and addresses them only as 'my in-laws'. He is shy in the presence of those who are grown-up to talk to them much. But he plays games with the little ones; he must not beat them in any circumstances.

RELATIONSHIP TERMS

If the mother of a child dies and she has a grown-up elder sister this elder sister takes her baby younger sister to take care of her and give her milk, her own breast-milk, and she gets strong and grows; and the husband of the elder sister hoes a cultivation in her name so that she may become strong with it. When she is grown up enough to marry a man she speaks of her elder sister as 'mother' ['*nai*'] and 'my mother' ['*nina*'], and she calls her elder sister's husband 'father' ['*buba*']. The husband of the younger sister calls him his in-law ['*gbioni*'] because he hoed a cultivation to her name.

GRANDMOTHER

Mother: 'o my son you go tomorrow to your grandmother.'

Son: 'o my mother, I am not going to grandmother's.'

Mother: 'o my son why do you say you will not go to your grandmother?'

Son: 'eh my mother, last time I went to grandmother's, grandmother was nasty to me.'

Mother: 'eh my son, you go and let her bless you. You, when it is daylight your father will be ready to go. So you go with your father, and your grandmother will bless you, for the ghosts can be troublesome and when they seized me I became obese. As she is an old woman, what do you hold against her, for she will soon be dead, so what harm would she do you? So, your grandmother is fond of you, I will put my message into your mouth and you will go and tell it to my mother, for I am in poverty and if she has something let her give it to me here. O my son do not sleep there, you must return the same day. That thing which my mother may think of giving to me, she can give it to you to bring back with you for me.'

Son: 'o my mother, that mother of yours, she will get the better of you. I will go lest you say I refused. There are people with grandmothers who do not trouble them as mine does me. I will go tomorrow to visit her and if she has some nice thing I will steal it. She can object, but no matter. Eh my mother, that journey I went with you to grandmother's, her dried meat was there and we came home beside it.'

Mother: 'eh my son do you not make things up!'

IN-LAW BEHAVIOUR

In-law behaviour, which is that when a man visits his in-laws, is the same as when a man visits the court. When men go there they avoid the kind of way in which they behave at home. If a man is rather careless about how he wears his bark cloth in his own home,

when he goes to his in-laws he takes with him his fine bark cloth
to wear it there and to look proper in it. If it is that he is a loud
talker he tones down his voice and answers his mothers-in-law
with a soft 'yes'. And his idleness also, even if he is very lazy in
his own home, when he arrives at his in-laws he hides his laziness
and works hard so that his mothers-in-law speak well of him. And
hunting also, if he hears of a hunt he hastens to the place with his
in-law's net. Eating also, a man does not want to break off a large
lump of porridge into his mouth in the presence of his in-laws nor
gulp it down quickly in their presence. An in-law eats his meal
slowly, so they do not put him together at a meal with children;
so the in-law eats by himself.

And if he comes with spears to fetch his wife he comes and
hides them in the bush—maybe some four of them—hides them
near the path as he approaches his in-law's home. Then he rests
for a long while, and they kindle the evening fire and they take
his stool and place it by the side of the fire (for in the past people
had stools or couches for their in-laws). They came and sat with
their in-laws beside this fire, those who were the elder sons of the
home (and any who came with him) around the fire.

When the in-law sees it is getting dark he gets up and goes off to
fetch his spears to speak about them. He rises and squats before
his father-in-law and speaks thus 'my father, this "ring" [these
spears] I have brought for you; who has no father says he has no
father; my father died long ago; so I have brought you just a
"ring"; do not be angry with me, for I am a poor man and there
is no one to help me. I have no sister after me [whose bridewealth
would have come to me], so it is only you my father-in-law to
whom I can make appeal to let me have my wife. I have no kinsman
to give me spears. My father's younger brothers are against me,
they have all severed kinship with me. My father long ago dispersed the bridewealth when I was a child, and when I grew up I
found that father had distributed all the bridewealth among those
younger brothers of his. Not one of them said that as I was poor
he would give me some of the bridewealth of his daughters since
my father was very good to them to give them the bridewealth
of my sisters; and now that he is departed in death not one of
them has helped me, not one of my father's kinsmen has done
anything for me. So my father-in-law, I tell you about my poverty,
that I married by my exertions.'

His father-in-law replies 'yes sir, we also have in our time married wives and we know all about how it is—just a few spears, just a few in the path of marriage—let no one say that I begat a daughter that a man should pay her bridewealth all at once to give it to the father of the child. If you seek for the spears one by one and bring them, there will be no objection, for I understand all about your poverty. Spears are like a rubbish-heap—if you bring them one by one they increase and grow large.' He says 'child you hand me those spears.' He takes them in his hand and taps them on the ground [to test them], and then he says 'all right, they are good [heavy] spears; child,' he says 'go and put them in the hut.' He says 'go and call my sons. 'The eldest of them comes and sits near his father. His father says 'yes, my son, I have called you so that you may come and hear about these spears of your sister's husband. When I die people may dispute about the spears, so I am going to count his spears in his presence. He has given me fifteen spears, I say that clearly and you have heard it.' He shows assent. 'The fifteenth of them is what he has brought today, that which the boy has put in the hut just now. Come tomorrow morning and look at it [them].' He says 'child, call her [his daughter's] mother.' Her mother comes and the elder says 'it is I who have sent for you to speak to you about your daughter, to say that she has been here long enough so you must take her back now with him, for this is what he has come for.' The son-in-law thanks him [sweeps the ground in front of him] and rises and seats himself.

His mother-in-law then says 'good, she accepts her husband's wish, as I have said before'—that is, if she is a well-disposed mother-in-law. 'But her hair must be plaited tomorrow. Let him wait for her, her hair must be plaited first, a girl must not go back to strangers with her hair all awry.' The elder say 'o you, you have got all that from your mother, it is not what I say.' He [the husband] says 'all right, I will wait for her hair to be done but don't let it be too long doing for elephants are near our home and will eat it all up, and if they get into the home they will eat all the bananas and destroy all the granaries. And what manioc they see when they come they will eat it all up. That manioc your daughter planted has indeed flourished by her home.' The mother-in-law says 'all right, you will not have to wait long. It won't be many days for otherwise your food-plants might suffer from animals, you will only wait two days and then you can go home.' The elder says 'all right, but since you are bad at putting things off let it not be more than the two days you have promised.'

MOTHER-IN-LAW

'O my mother-in-law, you are quite well mother?' [Mother-in-law]: 'you have come to find me at my work. I am really exhausted with the work.' [Son-in-law]: 'o my mother, goes all well mother? My mistress I have been longing to see you. Oh, that my mother-in-law has come today has made it an altogether happy day for me. O mother! You say that I married a wife—I married her because of you mother!'

'Yes my son, I was moved by love of my child and I thought I would come to visit you. I have had bad trouble over there and I have been very sick husband to my daughter.'

'O my mother what has been troubling you over there which is bad trouble? My mother how is my father-in-law?'

'He is well sir and he sends you his greetings. I thought I would spend one night here, but it is the season of work so then I must get back to the cultivations of my home.'

'Very good my mother-in-law, you spend some time with us first and then you return.'

When a farting person farts like *tu* people hear the sound of it, but if he farts *faya* his mother-in-law does not hear it and so it does not matter. If a man farts in the presence of his mother-in-law but gently and if he does it in the company of many persons his mother-in-law cannot know that it was he. It is the farting person who farts *tu*, it is he who gets much shame. If a man farts in the presence of his mother-in law when they are alone together and the mother-in-law is embarrassed, then, if he has a knife he takes the knife from his waist and places it before his mother-in-law, saying 'o my mother-in-law a misfortune has befallen me, o my mother-in-law it is from God. O my mother-in-law there is nothing I can say.' The mother-in-law is so overcome with embarrassment that she does not laugh. She takes the knife. If there are unrelated people present these unrelated people are likely to relate it to others as a piece of gossip, saying that a man farted in the presence of his mother-in-law; so they may gossip about it. It is like this, master, Azande say that when a man goes to visit his mother-in-law he wears his bark cloth and arranges it, and then he sits well and firmly, and he must not wriggle lest he fart in the presence of his mother-in-law and be put to shame.

ABOUT MYSELF (TITO)

This is about my troubles, I Tito. Now, when I was a child and had not grown enough to fend for myself that grandmother of mine who bore mother, her home was in [Prince] Ngere's province. So while I was small, when my father went to consult the poison oracle he took with him a chicken for me, and he said to the poison oracle that since he had begotten my sister and me, the two of us, should we go to visit our maternal uncles, they being our kin; if misfortune would beset us there, then let the poison oracle kill the fowl. But if this was not true, nothing bad would happen to us there, let the poison oracle spare the fowl. The fowl died, saying that if we went there somebody would die in consequence.

Well, after a long time we were forgetful. Well, one day grand-mother came and when she was leaving I had a desire to go with her and we went off together with her to my maternal uncles' home. We stayed there a short while when Udibasia collected police (*asekere*) at the fort and sat with them there and took one of them from among them who was a kinsman of this grandmother of mine, and they went to reside at Ngere's and there began to plan to shoot animals. This maternal uncle of mine told me that I should accompany him in the bush because he had no boy at hand. I agreed to go with him, and grandmother raised no objection to our going off together, so we went off into the bush together and we ate much meat. So we continued on our way to Tali's country where abscesses began to seize my throat, and I became so ill that I nearly died. So we had to return to Ngere's province, to grandmother's home. It was though it were death; so I went to the home of that maternal uncle of mine, Ndili. He went to consult the poison oracle, and he took a fowl and asked the poison oracle if it was something where I had been that caused my sickness, then kill the fowl. That was not the case, it was someone at home, then poison oracle spare the fowl. So the poison oracle told him that it was his wife Nagu, it was she who said that, as grandmother had said that someone might go and look for game, let him be sick. So they came and told her this and she came and blew water over me, saying that if it was her witchcraft I would get well. Now, another maternal uncle, Ngbasuma, took a knife and lanced the abscesses with it and the pus gushed out. So they sent a messenger to my parents to hasten hither, telling them that since I went to my maternal uncles I was dying. So my fathers arose, also my mothers and my elder brothers [by a different mother], to hasten and they came and saw me. This thing which had burst, they said about it that they would not leave me or I would soon be dead there; for the poison oracle had in the past said that one of us would die at our maternal uncles' home. So my maternal uncle agreed, and my fathers carried me from there and brought me back to the east here, and they bathed the wound frequently and it began to heal. That is what happened to me, that I was sick almost to death, that was the misfortune which troubled me. Also I had a wound in the sole of my foot and I was very ill indeed from this wound. These misfortunes fell on me.

CAMP[1]

When a man goes to make a new homestead he first goes to reside in a temporary camp-hut called *bataya* and leaves the building of the new home to be done later. He says to his relatives 'you say I don't help you, well, I have come back, for I have endured much ill-fortune. If anyone had died there you would have said that I am a bad man.[2] So I tired much of it all, and I said that if I were to die among strangers it would be as if I had no kinsmen.'

He sent a boy with this message to his kinsmen. He spoke it to the senior of them: 'said my father thus, he is returning to reside among you. Said my father thus, have not my wives died, all of

1. This text is obscure. One has, as it were, to read between the lines, and this is easier to do in Zande than in English. It does, however, illustrate the deception, suspicion, animosity and bickering only too obviously (to one who has lived with Azande) among close kinsmen. It also illustrates what I have said about *sanza*, the innuendoes and hidden meanings as in so much of Zande conversations.
2. He had left his relatives and then came back and told them: 'well, you see I have come to live near you.' He speaks of his brothers whom he took with him.

1. Two girls

2. Boys' circumcision dance

3. Young girls

4. Women beating Eleusine for a Feast

them? This is why I am returning to you, or my children may
all die and be finished, and then you would say it is I who insisted
on remaining for ever in that place.'[1] He was just deceiving them;
things had gone ill with him in that place, so he was coming back
to his kinsmen.

One of the men replies to what the boy has said: 'all right my
son, that is very good. He told you to come and tell me what I
am to do. Did I come with you?' The boy replies 'father that is
your affair, if you want to act thus that is your affair.' The elder
changes his tune: 'you go and say to him that I will come tomorrow; only that coming of his to see me at our home here—he
delays on the path—that is indeed perplexing to me. You go and
tell him that I will come to see him tomorrow.'

The boy goes to where his father is in camp, and he says to his
father 'my father, I went and told it to him and he said he would
come tomorrow.' When the boy had spoken this speech he remained silent. His father bowed his head to think the matter over.
He was silent not speaking a word, and then he rose among the
people and returned to his place beside his little fire. He called one
of the older men to come and consider the matter with him. He
asks him 'friend, that business those men are putting across me,
friend what shall we do on our side?' His old wife, with whom he
started his home, pricks her ears up towards where her husband is.

He goes on to say 'why does he treat us with so much deceit?'
The other replies, the one he called into consultation, 'friend,
early tomorrow morning we must leave this place. This man is no
kinsman of ours; he would drive us into the bush.' He replies
'friend, you, let us sleep and when the morning star appears in the
east we will leave here, for he has treated us very ill.' His old wife
overhears this whispered plan and she says 'I speak out, for all
the women are away in the bush collecting firewood. I said I would
speak to this man, but he pays no attention. Just look at it! He is
his old full brother! How could a man's kinsman treat him like
this!' The other man says 'you hold your tongue lady. This is a
matter for men.' It remains like that till he says to his friend, 'you
leave off friend, you go away, you go away. That woman is not
agreeable with her talk.' He rises and takes his spear and departs
for his home. As he moves aside he says to him 'friend, come here.'

1. 'That it was I who went away with the children and that is why they
 died there.'

He comes after him to the path and comes and stands beside him. 'Friend, you tell me that please, you tell me that please.' He says 'friend, this is not real kinship, this is not real kinship. He has turned people against us; so he said that if we return we might speak a debt against him.' He replies 'my younger brother, be silent, be silent. However, you will know all about it, you will know all about it. When I summon you, you come after me in the night.' The younger brother begins to lose patience with him: 'hm, my friend, when you went with straight talk you got there. Now you go and talk children's talk to me.' The elder brother turns with real anger and says to him 'friend, you had better go to sleep.' Then he goes for good. His younger brother bids him good-night. He acknowledges the salutation with a double-talk grunt—'hm!'

They sleep until the elder brother wakes from sleep. He says 'hm! Hm! Hm! You there, give me that tobacco of mine over there.' He speaks to his wife and she brings it to him. He prepares his pipe and inhales the smoke. He then says to his wife 'bring my things out of the hut; I am going to call that man over there.' He calls to his younger brother 'you there, you are still asleep! You there, you are still asleep!' For his part he comes to deceive him: 'you there, when troubles come upon people, does a man break his neck with sleeping in the bush?' He replies 'I am up sir, I have long been up. Let us go. Let us get going. That mother's son of ours is coming after us this morning.' They rise and collect their things in haste and they begin to walk off.

The other man comes to look for them in their place in vain, for he sees no signs of them at all. He gets on their tracks and follows them and sees them where they are resting. He talks to himself as he goes along—'does not a man, even though he gets older, keep to all his bad habits!' This man bows his head and refuses to speak at all. He says nothing.

Their blood-brother says to them 'wo! Wo! You there, oh, what business have you done with our affairs there? When you come to my home you go on doing it.' 'Master, I am just sitting here. What do you mean by mediating between us? I saw the sun before he did.[1] I am just waiting here to die. And if I die let them bury me in the earth by myself.' The man who came says 'so, let us go, you get up and let us go.' He wanders off along their path and goes. The other says 'he he, son of my mother, o! Have you not

1. 'I am the elder.'

come to see me?' The blood-brother says 'friend, since you did not take the precaution of consulting your rubbing-board oracle, what can you say about it?' He then keeps silent and it is finished. They are at peace, and there is no more trouble.

MEN ADDRESS THE GHOSTS AT THEIR NEPHEW'S SHRINE

'O my son may no ill befall you. May your home be peaceful. When you take a wife may they not return your marriage-spears. May marriage affairs go easy with you. My son may you not throw your spear just into the ground, but may you spear an animal mortally. O my son may you prosper. I am older than your father and if his ghost is with me it is well with me. I bless you. You don't look after me. You pay no attention to what an elderly man wants. When I have gone may your hunting flourish. Those witch-crafts which trouble you, I withdraw mine from them my son to leave your hunting for those who hate you. Mistress of the home, you have married a man; you eat your meat. O wife of my son you honour me madam! When I have gone may animals die into the pot of my shrine.' The mistress of the home replies 'yes father, think of those other wives; if it were me my animal would be killed right away and I would eat it.'

A younger uncle of her husband joins in: 'his father protected him with *bagbuduma* medicines, and anyone who interferes with our hunting will indeed suffer from the medicines in his body.' Then he takes his magic whistle to blow on it, saying 'that witch who comes to spoil my son's hunting, he dies. My son's wives, you have heard it; and now I have finished what I have to say.' Then he blows out salt, saying 'my son, may you increase like salt. May you not abate; may your seed [children] not decrease. We do not throw spears into the ground. We shall not miss with our spears.' His son answers 'it is true. If I find a good hunting area I shall not fail to kill. I shall hunt well father.'

A MATERNAL UNCLE'S CURSE

A maternal uncle sees a nice thing belonging to his sister's son and he says to him 'my sister's son, please give me that nice thing.'

Maybe that thing is something like bark cloth. The sister's son replies '*ai* uncle I will not give it to you, I have only one of it.' The uncle says 'o my sister's son you do not do well with me about things. In the past I saw you had a spear and I asked you for it since my sister wearied herself bearing you, and likewise you did not do well with me. So it is that seeing bark cloth I asked you to give it to me. My sister's son if you do not give it I will blow on my breast to you. I will test you with the breast indeed—you are not compassionate towards your mother who bore you. You treat your mother with indifference.' The sister's son says 'sir, you should give things to me since you gave birth to me, and what nice things have you ever given me? I will not for my part give my bark cloth.' The uncle replies 'all right my son.'

The uncle goes home and arrives there and sits down and says 'my sister gave birth to bad children here who do not bear me in mind. I might not be their mother's brother for they do not respect me; now one of them has treated me ill over bark cloth also. Alas it is as if my sister had not borne him. May he not kill animals; may his first crops not flourish; may he not with the curse on him marry a maiden, may he marry only old women with that strong maternal curse; whenever he goes to make a case at court may they not give the verdict in his favour. Alas, that son of my sister, may he not become rich, his home will be despised.' He says further 'he gives his feast and rain will soak it. Alas, just this one breast which is on my chest, which is on the chest of my sister, for the breast from which he sucked is the same as mine; I am going to make ill his fate with it.' He takes his breast in his hand, saying 'o my sister's son have you not treated me ill? May your affairs not go well with you.' He blows on his breast: 'o my sister's son you will speak like a fool.' [He beats his belly and says] 'below my belly is that of my sister which gave birth to you.' Such is the curse of a maternal uncle.

WIVES OF SONS MOCK THE CORPSE OF THEIR FATHER-IN-LAW

When an elder dies the wives of his sons take a winnowing-basket in their hands and hover with it beside the corpse of their father-in-law, chanting 'mother oh, mother oh, just an aged fellow has died oh.' Someone says 'well, maybe he is dead, but he long ago begat husbands for them.' But the girls speak in mockery, saying 'he just died of old age.' The sisters of the dead say 'eh! No oh! You mock his corpse on account of his being old. If he were still with us we would see him and be happy, for all his kin had died and he was an elder all on his own.'

[The wives of sons]: 'hm! Oh ho! Alas, an old man has died all right. Hm! He stinks, he stinks, he stinks.'

[The sisters]: 'you talk like that! Won't you fathers die? All right, you talk away—you will die too. If unrelated people were to mock our dead like you do something pretty serious would happen. You can talk like that because you are wives of sons.'

[The wives of sons] 'He! He! What will you do to us? What will you do to us? No oh, he killed someone [by witchcraft]. He bewitched a cultivation.'

[The relatives]: 'if he had bewitched a cultivation, then vengeance-magic must decide the issue.'

A MOTHER-IN-LAW ADDRESSES THE GHOSTS AT HER
SON-IN-LAW'S SHRINE

When a man's mother-in-law blows out water on his shrine she speaks thus 'you ghosts, since this man married my daughter he behaved very well at first, but then he took to beating my daughter all the time and I did not like it at all. I said to myself "so, are we not mothers of children? It is not good that a man should marry your daughter and then everyday you hear her cries." So it is—he beats my daughter in this way and I do not like him for it at all. I say let him stop beating my daughter all the time, let him just admonish her with his mouth. We are mothers of children—if you must strike my daughter do not close your fist to strike her with it, let your hand be loose and open to slap my daughter with it thus; otherwise trouble comes of it; for we who are mothers wearied ourselves in bearing children; so you will say that that man who makes my daughter miserable, if he treats her like this, love of his marriage-spears may melt away. Although that is how I see it I said to myself "oh no, I won't act like him," and that is why I rise and take water to blow it at his shrine. May they be at peace. Words which I think always and speak inside myself are affecting them in their home with that grindstone she brought by herself to her home;[1] if it is that which is causing them trouble in their home, so then I have risen and blow water at their shrine that they may be at peace, *phsia* . . .'[2]

WOMEN ERECT A SHRINE

[A man consults the rubbing-board oracle]: 'as I am going after that mother of mine to summon her, will my shrine be successful—I will kill animals, marry many wives, and be on good terms with all men? Oracle stick!' The oracle sticks [answers in the affirmative]. 'Shall I chop *doma* wood [for the shrine]?' The oracle answers 'no'. He asks the oracle 'shall I chop *sasa* wood?' The oracle answers 'no'. He asks the oracle 'shall I chop *bombili* wood?' A good oracle seizes in favourable consent.

[The wife of the home goes to get her husband's mother to address the ghost of her husband's father in her home.] She says: 'old woman, you give me porridge. Oh mistress! You have long been old, an old person does not eat things like that.'

'Eh! Wife of my son, leave the food in my mouth, then may I not die!'

'He! Eh mistress! You have already finished with food. He! This old woman, what is she waiting for that she does not die?'

'*Ai!* O my mistress lady! Did they tell you that one person cannot die at the same time as another, lady?'

'He! To where will you flee from death?'

'Eh! And did I not bear a husband for you lady? And you turn me towards the earth for death.'

'He mistress! You play with your son. You are going, my mother, to him.'

[The husband's mother speaks at the shrine]: 'thus, o my son Kisanga you do me ill. When you kill a beast you do not give mother its stomach. I feel hurt because of that. O my son, since we are together, why my son when you kill animals do you not give me meat my son? That medicine here [at the side of the shrine] —may Kisanga appear in the places of the corpses of his animals; may he marry his wives; may he not fight with spear-shafts. But

1. She brought the stone by herself, that is, she was not accompanied to her husband's home. There was some irregularity.
2. The sound of water being blown out.

so I give up. You medicine, you show spirit as good medicine to give judgement in favour of Kisanga. O my son it is your fault—you kill beasts, you should give of them to your mothers. But we won't go on with this thing any more today, for we have come to bless you, to bless you from our hearts. My son, witchcraft may get you into trouble with the princes or with the Europeans, and people may say that it is on account of your mothers, that we who are your mothers have cursed you. My son, since we leave off the matter . . . O my son, you give up being miserly; you be generous to us. You, medicine, which is here, we put you at the side of the shrine here and close the shrine with you. When he sees his animal may he spear it strongly. O my son, for we are very fond of you, for your father died and left you in our care. O Kisanga, since you bear our relatives in mind, about what do we come to erect a shrine for you? And then the ghosts are ill-disposed to us together with you. Your mothers have said that since your father died it is for us to erect your shrine. O my son there is no double feeling towards you; if there were I would not have come. Your father liked me best of all among his wife's younger sisters; and I want his ghost to be kind to me. O Deleakowe are not the ghosts with God? If you favour me as you favoured me in your lifetime! Since you died leaving your son, your son has been very unhappy, for his kinsmen dislike him. O our father, our husband, give us fortune together with your son so we may praise the ghosts and say that the ghosts judge well. Since you died things have gone ill with your offspring, he has not begotten children. It would seem that the ghosts refuse him a child. May he beget a child after this blessing with which we have come today to bless him.

'Eh my son! Leave off childish things—the princes are well disposed towards you and the Europeans too. When you go to marry a wife may she not refuse you in your home. I am a last-born child who dried up the mother's milk, for I am the child who brings to an end, and therefore I am able to erect shrines for all of you. Those things I have in my heart, I give them all up my son. I give them all up. O my son you have no energetic wife. My son, if you marry an energetic wife your home will be like your father's was. You sit in your misery my son to die in your misery my son. And may you have not desire for another's possession. Leave a man's wife to him, for when a man's father is dead and he starts that sort of thing, he who is an orphan, to make trouble, he will not long survive his father. Well, your father married you a single wife. You stay with her to ponder the words of your father —when a father dies strangers are no good. O my son do not play with princes and do not leave the path of the Europeans, for, my son, the Europeans are kings. O my son, as I am erecting a shrine for you, you bear in mind also our welfare who are your mothers. If it had just been your father he would not have seen you my son. It is woman—a man marries a woman first sir and then his son will see offspring. Your mother wearied herself much with you in her womb. So my son, she journeyed with you all over the place to search for medicines for sickness, for the *Amadi* sickness [of babies] . . .'

Her elder sister cuts in with 'mistress to what purpose do you weary your mouth with repetition? Does he ever think of our welfare? He thinks that he is clever, that he begat himself. I say that if he thinks this it will bring upon him the ill fate of his mother's resentment. So, for a child should not bear ill-will towards his mother. My son, we erect for you a shrine today, for a man's mother gives him a blessing; you take our goodwill which is blessing on you my son. My son, do not beat your wife, do not quarrel with your wife my son. My son, a wife is good. For if a man does not marry a wife he does not see offspring, his seed my son. If your mother had been barren then our husband. . . . My son, she thought how to bear you on the marriage-spears. But my son she was fruitful. If your wife makes trouble for you with witchcraft and you think your mothers have cursed you, we will not any more; we altogether abandon the curse. Give me cold water lady for me to blow it on him to remove mine, or his fathers are going to say it is because it is we who are his mothers scold him that he is unfruitful, for ill-fate following resentment is not good. One does not argue with a mother. O ghost of Deleakowe you do not see my unhappy son sir, otherwise why would you spoil the hunting nets of your son? The great epidemic which has fallen on the world, may it not seize your son, for he is the only surviving one of your sons. O ghost of his father, that is why we have spoken to you today. As I have admonished him, so when I have gone let him do it [what I have told him]. My son I am an old woman who has come to bless you today, for I am of those from whom bodies you came.'

Family, Kin and In-Laws

'You! You! Since I put you here I put you among good things and you will go on eating them when I am no longer alive. A man does not reprove the son of another on the track of a big reed rat. A man reproves only his own son, mistress. As I am about to depart, be energetic, let your hand be strong; don't let your fire go out by sitting over those of your friends; when you get up and say that you will not be by your fireplace, your fireplace— the grasses will grow around it and your friends will laugh at you. When I first had my fireplace I was not like you. I was just a small little thing. Whenever I cooked a meal it was too much for me, and it was my husband who came to teach me; but you are grown up. A woman says that I roast a little thing and do not give it to my husband—o wife of my son I have heard it, I have heard it; that is a bad business mistress—if you do him ill it will hurt me. You come from a different clan, you separate out your affairs.

'When you rise in the morning place water before your husband right early in the morning. Pluck *nzawa* leaves, do not let him wash [dry] his face with his hands. Do not urinate in the hut and do not urinate on the bank of earth round the courtyard because of the vegetables. You are a human being, so go far to the cultivations to do what you have to do there. Now that you have come to be wife to my son do not be haughty with him in the sleeping-hut. So, if you refuse him in the sleeping-hut he will go after a man's wife, and that means payment of compensation. The wife who gets angry with her husband it is that wife a husband beats and for that. Do not separate from him on the bed and go and sleep on the ground over there. So, as I am introducing you to the home, you sleep with your husband. You draw water and put it on the fire, and then you get up and your husband will wash himself with the water—you will wash him all over; a wife washes her husband's penis, that is the custom.

'You get up to go to your father's home and your husband follows after you, do not show your distaste or he will think that you have another man in the bush, so he will be hostile to you on that account. Firewood, firewood, mind you go and gather plenty of firewood, plenty of firewood, o my son's wife do not

sleep in the dark, darkness is not good. When you cook something
put plenty of fire to it or it tends to be undercooked, because if
you serve something more or less raw to a husband he dislikes you
for it; raw things are not good. When I married your husband's
father I had not many habits lady! All your husband's things—his
beer—do not go and show where your husband's things are to
people; people are not good, they are capable of killing him for
beer. When he kills an animal for you, you dry it inside the hut;
do not dry it outside where people can see it, for if a man sees it he
goes off to tell about it to other men. The cause of your death
can begin on account of seeing a beast with the eye. Wife of my
son you must hide things. His friends come to sit with him, his
bachelor friends, then break off two lots of porridge wife of my
son, for you should take his and put it away; and when the men
have dispersed you take this small helping of porridge which you
put in the hut and give it to your husband. It is the habits of women
I am speaking to you about lady. That little cooking oil, do not
eat it up on the grindstone. Because you have a little salt do not
let your friends get round you for you to give it to them. When
you have gone and given them that salt your husband goes and
kills your large beast and you will cry out in sorrow, wondering
where you will find salt now; it is you who will have brought
misery on yourself lady. If you hide your little bit of salt from
women, saying that you have no salt, then you will not suffer
unhappiness. Do not show dislike for the wives of your husbands.
Do not show dislike for your husband's younger brothers. Do not
complain and talk ill of people lady. That is witchcraft, it has the
same character. When your husband hoes a cultivation for you do
not squander it, take good care of it [the fruits] from women. A
woman leaves her thing and comes and eats of yours and then goes
home to eat up her own too. You, do not serve food with spit.
See that he has plenty of food, for you are an elder's daughter,
the daughter of one of the best families [*mbomu*]. When you go to
a stream to fish by ladling out the water, do not hide the catch
from your husband. Do not insult people; I don't like insults; and
people will not come to your home lady. Be open-handed thus, be
open-handed to people thus, and people will come. Get up while
it is scarcely light, right early in the morning to go and hoe your
cultivations lady. Do not go on sleeping when it is dawn. Always
get up early in the morning; a good wife gets up at cock-crow. I

leave off. I will say no more now; I shall wait to see how you shape, lady.'

SUICIDES

Some people kill themselves with iron [knives or spears], others with cord. What prays on a man's mind so that he kills himself on account of it is shame. There are people who cannot abide shame, shame is a frightful thing to them. A shame which afflicts a man is this: the accusation of something of which you are innocent. You deny it in vain for no one pays any attention to your denials. You give oracular tests in vain, they still hold it against you, and they want to injure you everywhere. It preys on your mind greatly; it appears that your kinsmen have deserted you. You feel hurt, and you decide to kill yourself with cord. That terrifies them afterwards. It shows them that you were innocent of what you were accused of. They become angry among themselves and turn against him who started these stories about you without cause.

Another cause of shame is that your relatives accuse you of theft and show ill-will to you. You deny it vainly, they continue to show ill-will to you, and they do not want you in their homes. They call you thief in public. When they have thoroughly shamed you you want to kill yourself so that they may know by that that you never stole anything. That being so, you kill yourself with a gun, if you have one; if not, with a cord; for many people kill themselves with cord, because it is a quick death.

Another way of people killing themselves is by knife. A man kills himself with a knife because he is sick and is quite worn out by his sickness and totally emaciated by it; then he recovers. But then later it seizes him again and wears him out and he becomes totally emaciated as before. He is exhausted and he takes his knife and drives it into his naval and dies at once. Some men take a razor and cut their throats so that they die at once. That prince Mopoi who died some time ago [before 1927] endured illness for many months and he became emaciated so that it seemed to him to be too great a tribulation to bear. He took his razor [knife] which he had at his waist and stuck it into his navel and severed his navel cord, and he died at once. Another sickness which causes a man to kill himself is leprosy, for leprosy is a terrible disease which eats away all a man's toes and fingers.

A man who killed himself was the son of Basafuru, a subject of Gangura, though why he did so is unknown. He arose and wandered, but neither his father nor anyone else knew to where he had wandered. He went and stripped the bark off the *dakpa* tree [made cord from it], tied it above [to a branch] round his neck, and when he let go of the tree the cord tightened round his neck and he died at once. He was four days in the bush before anyone saw his corpse. His relatives thought he had gone on a journey. It was a woman who found his body in the bush and she told Gangura, and then his kinsmen went out and cut the cord above. No one knew why he had killed himself. They thought among themselves that he may have had relations with his sister and that he had taken his life from the shame of it. Others said that perhaps he had at some time killed a man and that he took his own life out of remorse, but no one really knew why he had committed suicide.

That which I [Kuagbiaru] saw myself at the mission station [C.M.S.] happened to the younger brother of a man there called Baliekuali. A crowd of the mission boys, including this younger brother of his, Maminzi, went on a hunt. After hunting, on their way home, a boy hit Maminzi's dog with the shaft of his spear. Maminzi flew at this boy to beat him really hard. His elder brother, Baliekuali, was angry at this and he abused him in the presence of many people, calling him 'uncircumcised'; for he was uncircumcised. He much resented this, and he said to his elder brother that on account of what he had said to shame him before many people he would og away to a far place and he would not see him again. When he had spoken thus he burst into tears with mortification. They continued on their way and arrived home, he in silence. When night fell all went to bed. Early next morning he walked to the Uze forest. He made [from bark] a stretch of cord, and he tied it above to the branch of a tree, placed the noose round his neck, and when he let go of the tree the cord tightened round his throat and he at once died. When people found his corpse they brought it home. Of all these things, what people mostly kill themselves for is shame. Those Azande who count honour high do not care to be shamed.

CHILDREN AND SEX

When desire for his love comes over a young man he goes to lie on his bed and pines for his love. If then he is by himself he begins to push on his mat (as on a woman).

And small boys for their part—one will take hold of another to press on to him in boys' play, but this is what he has seen his father doing, his father copulating with his mother—so he goes after little girls whom he knows to try to copulate with them. So when a little boy mounts a little girl the grown-ups just laugh, just laugh quietly and then pretend to be angry, saying to him 'eh child, from whom did you get that idea? Who told you to start that sort of thing in front of people? It is just a child's behaviour.' If there are any unrelated people present they look with a meaningful look, as much as to say that the child has seen this with his father and is imitating him.

INCEST

When a boy reaches puberty he may take his sister and with her build their little hut near his mother's home and go into it with his sister and lay her down and get on top of her—and they copulate. His father then begins to keep a watch on them to catch them at this and seizes him and gives him a good hiding and asks him what he means by going after his sister, she is his sister, has he seen people going to bed with their sisters? Then he is afraid. He keeps a look-out for his father and when his father is away he again takes this sister and they go and hide in the bush to copulate. When they know that their father is returning they get out of the bush. So people say about it that a man begins desire for women with his sisters. So people say that children are like dogs, for a boy will go after his own sister. After they have been stupid for a time, when they grow up they get a sense of shame and whenever they see their sister they do not think of going any more with her to the bush. A youth feels ashamed with regard to his sister, he would not see her nakedness any more. When he and his sister are travelling together and his sister goes to wash in water she moves a long way away into the bush to wash there so that her brother will not see her nakedness, for that is shameful. Since I have grown up, should I see my sister's nakedness I would compensate her [with a gift] for that is just children's play, I have long forgotten it; since I learnt sense I left off childish things; what I used to do with my sister when we were small we have given up.

Lovers and Adulterers

YOUTH AND GIRL

'O my sister, that girl who was here, did you notice her?'
'I saw her here just now.'
'If you go and search for her will you find her?'
'Yes, I will find her all right.'
'You tell her to come.'
She goes and tells her, saying 'my brother told me to tell you to come.'
'Which of your brothers is he?'
'You know him very well.'
'You go and tell him that I will come as soon as I can; I am afraid, my husband is around.'
She returns to tell it to her brother, saying 'she said that she would come soon.'
'You go again, I am going out.'
After that she brings her.
She says to her brother 'you go ahead to your home, I will come right after you.'
'You must both come together, you show her the way or she may go astray.'
The man goes ahead to his home and the woman follows after him but with guile, leaving the path the man went by and going by a different path, and she arrives where the man is.
His sister says 'I am going, I have brought her, there she is.'
They enter the hut. He says 'o my sister, sit on the bed. When I sent a message to you why did you not come?'
'It was because of that man, my husband, being present; as soon as he went out then I came.'
'My sister, I want to marry you. Would your father not consent to my marrying you?'
'My father said that he is going to give back his [her husband's] marriage-spears.'

109

'My sister, I want very much to marry you. You listen well. It is only you yourself who could make it difficult for me, if you are willing I will marry you.'

'I hate him [my husband]. I do not care for him at all.'

Then he lies with her. After that she says 'my brother I am going. That man [her husband] may look for me in vain, and he is a violent man.'

'All right, my sister, you go. But I want you to come again, so do not stay away long. Be on your way.'

'Yes sir.'

'O my sister come again, you are beautiful and charming indeed. That nasty man, you shall not marry him. Go now or he may beat you.'

LOVE AFFAIRS

If a woman much desires a man she speaks to her friend thus, 'my younger sister, I desire your husband, you let me have your husband.' If she has a nice disposition she says to her 'all right my younger sister, you come and make love to my husband.' She [the first woman] says to her [the other] '*ai!* My sister, people will hear of it.' The other replies '*ai!* I could not get you into trouble.' So she comes to make love to the other's husband. The wife says to her 'it is not well for a man to sit [have congress] with a girl if she does not give him food as well as love, for if she does not give food it is shamelessness. That husband of mine whom you see, when he sits with women, if their dispositions are not good he lampoons them in the songs he composes.' She acknowledges what has been said and goes after him. His wife sees it but she would not say anything because she knew all about it.

If a woman has a love affair with a man and he does not often give her nice things like rings and piastres also it is shameful; and the woman leaves him to go and make another love-pact with another man who will give her nice things.

If a woman sees a man on a path she says to her companion 'my sister, those men I saw today, did you notice them?'

'Yes, my sister.'

'Oh my sister! What fine men!'

'My sister, if a person were to have a love affair with that one, how would that be?'

6. Assembly for Prince Rikita's Feast

5. Youths

7. Daughters and wives of Prince Rikita

8. A man mutilated for adultery

'Yes my sister, if he attracts you greatly you have an affair with him, it is of no consequence, some people are attractive to a person.'

She says to her companion 'hm! My sister that other one is no good, he has a pasty body and nasty eyes, he is no good. My sister it is not well to have an affair with an unattractive man. You get a bad name to no purpose.'

'Eh! My sister it is better to get a bad name on account of a handsome man than on account of an ugly one.'

When a man has attracted a woman, if his wife has a hostile disposition, she waits until she has seen his sister, to whom she says 'o child of my mother! I want you to know that I greatly desire your brother. It seems that his wife is very jealous about him, that is why I am afraid about him; if you see him perhaps you will tell him what I have said.'

His sister on her part says 'all right my sister'. Then she adds '*ai!* My sister, what if you are a man's wife and get my brother into serious trouble, for he has no one to pay a fine on his behalf, for his fathers have all died, leaving him in the care of his [distant] father's elder brother.'

'*Ai!* My sister, I would not wantonly give a man away.'

'All right, I will tell him.'

'O my mother's child! Mind you keep it dark from his wife, she must not hear about it.'

She goes to tell him. When she sees her brother she says to him 'my brother, a woman inquired after you today, and she sent me after you so that when we would be alone together I might tell you about it.'

MAKING LOVE

This is about when a Zande wants to have intercourse with a girl. A youth who sees a girl who much attracts him would not think of just passing her by, for Azande surpass all other peoples in adultery. When he meets her on the path he says to her 'maiden, hello.' She returns his greeting 'yes, sir.' He asks her, 'my sister where do you come from?'

'I come from [Prince] Sasa's country sir.'

'Who then is your husband?'

She says to him 'my brother, sir, an old man brought his spears to

father. I never agreed to marry him at all, for he espoused me when
I was just a little girl and knew nothing about it. I detest him.'

'My sister, you who live in the provinces do not think well of
us who live in the government centre, why? You like those who
wear bark cloth which smells when they hang it up.'

'Sir, it is only those who are not used to the centre, it is only
they who dislike people of the centre.'

'Eh, my sister, then you would be kind to the likes of us?'

'*Ihi, ihi*' [giggles].

'My sister, don't waste time thinking of it; be nice to me and I
will thank you my sister.'

'*Ihi*, what is it you want sir? But I am afraid of those people of
yours who might be unpleasant [his wife].'

'Hm, hm, my sister, as for that, has anyone told you there is
someone there who follows me? What have people got to do with
you?'

She replies 'and sir, for my part I don't know where a person
could rest.'

'Hm, my sister, how can there be lack of a place? If you had
been agreeable we would already have entered a hut together. It
looks as though I shall die from desire for you my sister. It is you
who have been making delay. Strangers may come at any moment;
so if you would do me the kindness I could get away from this
main path here.'

She replies 'now I think I know of a suitable hut, you can lead
the way.'

'My sister, get going, let us go at once, come on let's get going.'
She acknowledges what he says. When he has gone quickly and
opened the door of the hut and entered it he pats a mat hurriedly
and places it on the bed. Then he comes out of the door and
beckons to her. Then he re-enters the hut and puts his head
through the entrance to see her. She comes and creeps round the
wall at the entrance and enters after him into the hut. She stands
by the door-posts. He says to her 'please come and sit on the bed.'
She goes on standing. He waits a little while and then gets up and
takes her by the hand and seats her on the bed. In doing these
things his penis rises inside his bark cloth[1] and becomes stiffly

---

1. The suggestion earlier was that the youth was one who wore shorts, to
which the word *roko* can in a general sense be applied. However, the
text seems to make it clear further on that he was wearing the usual
bark cloth skirt.

erect, standing up straight. As soon as he starts to lay her down on the bed she giggles, and then he stretches her on the bed. She lies right down and takes off her waist-cord and pubic covering.[1] He has already taken off his bark cloth. He [places his arms under her and] draws her to him, and then lies for a little while between her breasts, and then he places his penis between her thighs and pushes it forwards and backwards two or three times [to increase his excitement] and then he draws it out. She embraces him with her leg and he mounts between her thighs and tucks his hand under her head. Then she takes hold of his penis in her hand and inserts it into her vagina. When he stretches forward his whole organ goes in right up to its base. When he has copulated with her for a time she gets great pleasure from it. She begins to thank him, saying 'oh! My brother, oh! My brother, I like it. Hold yourself back in doing it [do not ejaculate too quickly]. Oh! My brother, how pleasant does your penis feel there. Make it very slow.'

Then she blows into his ear. When she has done these things to him he ejaculates into her. When it is finished he withdraws his organ from her vagina, and she takes her pubic covering and wipes his organ with it. He then rises and throws his bark cloth around him, and she on her part sits in nakedness, and they converse in whispers, and they may smoke together also. When desire for her takes hold of him again he draws her to him again. Then he gives her a *tarifa* in payment.[2]

ABOUT WOMAN

When a youth is resting and thinks of a girl with whom he has had an affair, if she is in a far-off place he begins to think of her,

1. The ordinary dress of women was a girdle supporting bunches of leaves before and behind. Some of the girls had taken to wearing a strip of barkcloth in place of the leaves.
2. *Tarifa*, a half-piastre, is Arabic. We must not misinterpret this transaction. It is not in any sense 'prostitution' but rather a variety of 'gift-exchange': the girl gives him pleasure, not for money but because she likes him and enjoys it, and he makes her a small gift, which, though it may be money, has a sentimental rather than a commercial value, in return. A girl would not feel humiliated by it being known that she had accepted money or some other gift, but she would be if it were known that she had not been offered any.

saying to himself 'alas, where will I see my love again? Where will I see my love again to play with her and to sleep with her also, since desire for her so troubles me?' When he remembers the ravishing with which he ravished her he begins to get an erection, as he recollects her body, sees her breasts there, and sees her beautiful eyes, so he begins to have an erection. If he is by himself he takes hold of his penis and presses it thus and presses it thus [gestures with hand: he masturbates]. It is the same with women. When a woman who has had an affair with a man is with her husband she thinks of her love-affair and she begins to sulk with her husband. When the husband says 'eh! Woman why is it that you refuse to converse with me? What are you thinking about inside yourself in my home here?' She seeks some little excuse to put her husband in the wrong. This looks bad to the husband. He says to himself that she does not treat him in this way for no reason; there is a man who has spoilt her so that she brings things against him without cause. He begins therefore to abuse and thrash her. She then commences a really big sulk with her husband, whereas it is really her lover whom she has not seen for long, he is the reason why she says something malicious to her husband so that they may quarrel about it.

DANCES

I [Reuben Rikita] went to Rikita's country, who is my father. While I was there a man gave a dance, whose name is Aramasi. I decided to go and watch this dance to learn for what it is that Azande dance so much.[1] I went with three of my elder brothers, together with some of my small younger brothers. We went and arrived at the homestead of the dance.

The master of the home gave us a place and we sat down. However, up to that time not many people had gathered, just children were playing at dancing. I called the master of the home and asked him about this his dance, why people had not come to it to take part in it. He said to me 'master you be quiet, you will see people

1. This naïvety is explained by the fact that Reuben was sent to the C.M.S. mission when he was still a small boy. He was not therefore very well acquainted with much of the Zande way of life. Dancing was frowned on by the mission.

right now.' I spoke to him thus 'as it is already late in the day should not some of them have gathered?' He replied to me 'master, I arose at daybreak and went to the settlement of Ogbo; and when I came back from there I went at midday to the settlements of Awagi and Daya, walking from end to end of them spreading the news of my dance to the people. However, when I walked thus I was not just walking, my little [magic] whistle was in my hand with which I walk around and blow it. That whistle belongs to great song-leaders and they go around with it, that is those who want to open their dances for people to dance. It is the whistle of dances, that whistle which summons crowds of people to come to their dances. However, when I went through the settlements I told all the youths about the dance. Some of them told me "we have already heard the dance-gong, that which you beat in the morning." I said to them "all right, I am most eager to dance today.' He got up from our side and wandered off. We waited but a little longer and then the people of Ogbo's settlement came in large numbers, all with their girls also. They began serious dancing and they sang fine songs.

The master of the dance stayed away for a short time and then he came to where we were and saluted us, saying 'the princes have waited long?' We assented to him happily. He then went to the homestead of the dance and mounted the gong there. All stopped dancing. He spoke to them thus 'it is I, I Aramasi, who am giving this dance today to lament my younger brother with it. So I beseech you that you lament my man [brother] properly. Do not treat my dance with disrespect. Do not abuse it, for it is to the home of a great song-leader [himself] that you have come to dance. Those song-leaders who are in charge of the singing, let them admonish their choruses well, that they may not contest the songs, that they may sing their songs each in his turn. If it be that the song-group of Yuru come to sing their song now let the song-group of Aramasi be silent at once and dance to the song of the Yuru song-group. Those who are the drummers, let them organize their drumming well, let them not struggle for possession of the drum but keep my dance orderly. Let Nambaga, who is leader of the drummers, beat the drum first, and when he has stopped then others can beat it. Let each of you take it in turn and not struggle for it [not dispute possession of the drum].' When he had finished this speech he blew his little whistle and spoke this spell, 'may my dance not be at all stiff, let it be relaxed for all taking part in it. May great numbers of people assemble for my dance. May ennui not overtake those taking part in my dance, let them all be untiring [light].' He then got down from the top of the gong. Balingbandali mounted the gong [to beat it] and Nambaga took possession of the drums, together with a man called Siani. The dance began in full swing. Many people began to come from the settlement of Awagi and the settlement of Daya, and the place became packed with the crowd of men, mixed with women and small children.

That which I began to understand was that men dance because of women, for when a little drizzle of rain fell all the women scattered and only the men went on dancing; but those who continued dancing were not many, most of them ran [for shelter] at the same time as the women began to scatter. When the rain stopped the women congregated again, and then the dance began to resound with great resonance. They danced till midnight.

It is the habit of the Azande to dance till midnight and then they think of women to copulate with them. A man presses against [touches] an attractive woman whom he desires, and they wander off amid this crowd of people. I saw a youth there who fondled a woman and the woman went on dancing and when she was passing him he put his hand down to her pubic covering [pudenda] and as soon as she withdrew [away from the dance] he went together with her. Then he looked up and saw me nearby watching him and he left her, for he had wished to tell her that they should go away to some other place that he might have intercourse with her. Azande are always dancing only on account of women, for if there were no women present the men would not dance at all. When Azande dance at night they do not wear their best bark cloth, just an old bark cloth, for they want to play with the women whom they want to ravish also. Only the toughest of them want to dance for the dancing's own sake. At daybreak the people had already gone to the stream to wash themselves and anoint themselves well with oil. They put on their best bark cloth to show off with it before the women. A man wears his bark cloth as stylishly as he can because he wants to surpass his fellows so that the women will have eyes for him alone. Among the Azande it is like this: if the women favour one man much more than his fellows they [other men] bear him ill-will on account of this; for they want the women to like them all, even if a man is more attractive than they. There is nothing so pleasant to Azande than a dance; the dance is the first of all their activities, for there they see many women.

YOUTH AND MAIDEN

'You, girl, are you married? Can I marry you?'

'Have you not noticed that those who get husbands, unlike me, are attractive? Can't you find nicer girls than me to marry! I am not married sir, men are put off by my poor looks.'

'O my sister, tell me the truth.'

'What do you want me to say?'

'O my sister you tell me straight how you feel about it.'

'What a game are you not having [you are only just laughing at me]? All right, if you are serious come and hear what my brother and my mother have to say about it, for my father is dead. Men are triflers. I have already been deceived by one of them who in the end would not marry me.'

'My sister, he had a wife, that is why he gave it up. As for me, I am poor [without one]; I would not think of not marrying you.'

'All right, but I don't run after men; so you had better ask my kinsmen first.'

'My sister, nowadays it is ladies who first give their consent. If a lady doesn't consent to a man he doesn't marry her. It is when ladies give full consent to a man first that you then go to her father.'

'Hm, then I will come and see your home. What you say is all right, but you must visit my mother, and then I will come to your home to pay you a visit.'

'If I am away for three days it is because I am going to visit my elder brother who is said to be indisposed. I shall be away three days and then I shall come back. Don't you leave your home for you people can't keep away from dances.'

A WOMAN MOURNS HER LOVER

When a woman mourns her lover she twines grass into a mourning belt. When she has worn it for about three days and sees some members of the clan of her dead lover she says to them 'o my friends, please remove my mourning-cord.' They reply 'all right, you have mourned enough, you have done well.' They say to her further 'one does not remove a person's cord for nothing, that is, the cord one wears to mourn the death of a man.' She replies 'all right.' She takes some small metal object and gives it to them. If her sister is also present she takes a small metal object to place it by her sister's side. A relative of that woman you had an affair with unties the cord and takes it and ties it on a *bakeikpa* tree and they take oil and anoint her body with it. All this is done secretly so that a man's wife does not hear of it. This is why people say it is a bad thing when you come to see your wife with a grass cord round her waist, for this may mean that secretly she is mourning her lover. That is why husbands do not like it. If a man sees his wife wearing a grass waist-cord he asks her squarely to reveal the name of the relative of hers who has died, for a woman mourns a lover by wearing a mourning-string.

YOUTHS CHAT AMONG THEMSELVES

Some youths are gathered together and one of them says 'friend, I copulated with a woman over there. It wasn't up to much, her vagina was just all too soppy.'

'O my friend, that is a nasty type of woman.'

'Friend, my sweetheart over there, she gives me a wonderful time. Her vagina is just like manioc porridge. It is like gum.'

They burst out laughing and they laugh and laugh.

'Friend, I copulated with a woman over there and I did not sleep a wink all night. She had congress with me ceaselessly till dawn.'

They burst out laughing again and they laugh and laugh.

'Friend, that pretty wife of so-and-so over there, I am overcome with desire for her!'

'Whose wife?'

'Friend, one does not mention everybody's names. Friend, you who mention people's names all the time at night, you have a worn-out shield in your hands [you run the risk that the man of whom you speak will come and fight you].'

'Friend, you have only seen the outside of that woman. She

has stretched her vagina with men [she has been with so many]. I have copulated with her and she is just saggy.'

They collapse with laughter and laugh and laugh.

'Friend, I copulated with a woman over there, a strapping big woman too, and she was not even pierced. Why was that?'

'Friend, that sort of woman has an obstruction.'

'Quite right my friend, I copulated with a woman over there who was just like that.'

THE CHEATING OF LOVE AFFAIRS

When a man comes from afar, a man with whom a wife has had an earlier love affair, he says to her 'o my sister, because I love you greatly, when I come to your husband's home you must say about me "he is my kinsman". You must find the name of a brother of yours who lives over there and call me by it.' She replies 'yes, you say well my brother, when you come I will tell my husband exactly as you say; I will say to him "this man, he and I are near kin."' Her husband asks him 'friend what is your clan?' If this man's wife is a Giti he says to him, 'sir I am a Giti.' The husband then says to him 'what is your father's name?' He replies 'my father's name is so-and-so.' He says to the husband 'my father was her father's younger brother, and he is dead; we are his children, for this wife of yours had already gone away when she was small and I have not seen her for a long time. That is why I said to myself that I would pay her a visit.' His [supposed] in-law says to him 'that is all right,' and he adds 'an in-law does not avoid the obligations of kinship.' After that the visitor sits down with the husband, and they eat together a fine meal; and while they are doing so the husband says to him cunningly 'do you know her old name?' But if he is her lover she has already told him 'if my husband asks you about my old name you must tell him that it is such-and-such.' When he has given the name correctly the husband says to himself 'it is all right, she is his sister.'

Well, after that the husband thinks to himself that he will ask his in-laws about this business to get it straight. After that the visitor eats well, and then for some two or three nights she always places warm water before him for his ablutions, saying 'I place warm water for my brother, for him to wash'; whereas he is an unrelated man and it is her lover whom she honours without her husband being aware of it. Then he departs to return home.

After he has departed and arrived home the husband rises and goes to visit his in-laws. He arrives and rests. When evening comes he says to his father-in-law 'my father-in-law, father, there is just one thing, a man came to my home and told me that my wife was his sister. I told him to explain exactly what was the relationship between them. He told me that he was the son of that in-law of mine who died and of whose death I have heard. I told him to say what was her old name, and he spake it. So I considered the matter and I said to myself "all right, an in-law does not deny the obligations of kinship. I will know whether he is telling the truth when I hear the truth from my parents-in-law." ' His father-in-law says to him 'my son, did he tell you what his name was?' He mentions the name the man gave. His father-in-law then says to him about it 'yes, I expect it is he, so there is really nothing at all to worry about, so return home. If it is the son of that in-law of yours of whom you have heard but have never seen, if it is he, you can come later to see him to recognize him.' The husband departs and returns to his home and remains there.

They send a message to him: 'that in-law of yours who came to your home, come and see him. If it was he you will see him in our home and recognize him.' The husband looks at him and he says 'my father-in-law it is not he.' His father-in-law says 'my son, that sister of yours, have you been to her home this year?' He replies to his father 'my father, I have not visited her home this year.' The father-in-law says *'wo! Wo!* O my son! It seems that an unrelated man came to deceive you, to say that he was your in-law. That man who has deceived you about your wife; bring him along so that we can see him, because we do not know him.'

WOMEN ARE STUPID

Women are stupid, they are like fools and children. They do not think deeply, their thought is shallow, like the tip of a little finger.

A man tells his wife what she must do and she consents to what he has said. Then she goes away, and another man tells her not to do what her husband has told her to do but something else, and she changes her way of looking at things, disobeying her husband and obeying her lover. Women are totally unstable.

A man tells his wife 'you do this, you do that' and she does it. This is the custom of men throughout the world. Well, if your wife disobeys you, you beat her. This is how it used to be, and should be. But now the White Man has come, and no man's wife will obey him. You beat your wife and she goes to the District Commissioner or the *mamur*[1] with ever so little a sore; and they ask her whether she wants to stay with her husband, and if she says she does not; well, that is sufficient, you do not see your wife again, though you paid spears for her. This is a great grievance to us who are Azande.

You ask what happened in the past, in the lifetime of (King) Gbudwe; well, in the past you took to yourself a wife and she was lazy, oh so lazy! You said to her in the morning 'I am going to my cultivations to cut wood, you follow after me with your hoe.' Well, you work and work and keep on stopping to look round to see if your wife is coming. You cut and cut wood, and the sun mounts high, and still she has not come. Well, you leave your work and return home, and you say to your wife 'you are lazy, why have you not come to hoe with me?' She is silent. He speaks again: 'you are lazy. What did I marry you for if not to hoe my garden? I gave spears to your brother with which he has married a wife. Well, am I not to see work for my spears?' Now, if she is a bad woman, she will say 'eh he! Eh he! Go and work in your cultivations yourself, you can work and work till the sun falls, but you will not see me.' Well, the man will not answer her again, but he will take a stick and beat her well. Then he will go with her to her brother's home and will explain to him why he has beaten his sister. He will reply 'yes, it is true, my sister was lazy. You have a good case, you did right to beat her.' And he will turn to his sister and say 'sister, you are a stupid person, why do you not hoe your husband's cultivations. He did well to beat you. Laziness is a bad fault.' Well, the man will wipe the ground in front of his brother-in-law [to thank him] and will depart with his wife, who,

1. An Arab official of the Anglo-Egyptian Administration of the Sudan.

if she is a sensible woman, will not again refuse to hoe in his cultivations.

A DREAM

A man dreams a dream about a woman, with whom he has not previously had relations, that he has intercourse with her. He awakes from this dream, awakes from sleep, and turns round on his bed so that his head rests where his feet had rested at the bottom of the bed and he lies down to sleep an uneventful sleep. As he is about to rise at daybreak he considers the dream he has dreamt. When he turned on his bed and slept with his feet at the head of the bed, then the woman about whom he had dreamt began to dream a dream on her part that she lay with him.

While the man is walking about he sees this woman and, since she liked him before, he begins to solicit her and she consents to his suggestions and he had congress with her. They sit together and flirt and he says to her 'o my sister, the dream has indeed spoken truly, for I dreamt that I sat with you and now I remember what happened in the dream.' She says to him 'a dream is a cunning person. I dreamt my dream also. I said to myself about my dream that it was mocking me, whereas dreams speak true. Just as you dreamt your dream I dreamt mine like the one of which you speak.'

Therefore Azande say thus: 'you dream a dream about yourself and a woman, that is to say, about a woman with whom you have had no previous relations, and then you must turn round and sleep with your head at the foot of the bed so that she may dream a similar dream on her part.'

There is another dream that a man may dream, that he is having sexual congress with his sister, that he is copulating with her as though she were an unrelated woman; and when he wakes up from this dream he says [to himself] 'was not the dream shameful! I have now ravished my sister in a dream.' He would not tell it to other people—at least a man with any sense of decency would not—but he keeps it to himself. Only a loose-tongued fellow would tell of this dream about himself and his sister so that it gets around that a man has ravished his sister in a dream.

LESBIANISM

Women get together and one says to another 'o my friend, you, why don't you like me mistress?' The other replies 'o lady, my mistress, why should I bear you ill-will?' The first says 'lady, come the day after tomorrow as I have a little something to tell you.' She replies 'eh lady, what is it that you do not now tell me? For unless you tell it to me now I cannot survive the night waiting to hear it!' [So the one tells the other] 'lady, I am greatly in love with you. O lady how shall we manage this horrible husband?'

'Hm! Do they keep all that watch on a woman lady!'

'Ahe lady, let us play a trick. You come after my husband and we will make a pact of love-friendship between us and he will think it is just a friendship between women, and you lady can pleasure me!' She adds 'early tomorrow you come with a little gift for him.'

Early in the morning she takes a gift, such as a spear, and she comes to visit the husband in his home. She says to the husband 'so, will you listen well to what I am going to say to you?'

'Lady, say what the lady has come to my home here for.'

'Eh sir, sir it is about my friend, master, I said it to myself sir that I would come to ask the "prince" about her; no man am I who could deceive you with a woman sir.'

He says 'o lady maybe I shall consent.'

'O sir by your head! O sir by your head! Let me have the woman sir. Sir I will grind her flour for her, and if she is sick I will gather her firewood and her water.'

'I must consult the oracles first lady, I must consult the oracles first. I think I must first consult the oracles.'

'Eh sir, does one refuse with a woman? Is she a man?'

'All right my friend, you leave the spear and go home and I will think the matter over.'

She wipes the ground before him, saying 'o my master I go about by myself among people sir!' Then she goes home. She sleeps two nights and then grinds flour, and she comes to deceive with flour and porridge. When she appears on the path her lover runs to meet her on the path: 'o my love, o my sister, o lady have you not come today?' She puts down the flour and porridge at the side of the homestead. Her lover takes a stool and puts it for her to be seated. The husband sulks, 'you have come my friend?'

'Yes sir.'

'Lady let me be, I am feeling chilly today.'

They take his food and bring it. He is embarrassed: 'child come and pour water over my hands.' His wife goes and takes water and pours it over his hands. He says 'lady this is good, it is good.'

He breaks off one lump of the porridge. He sulks and goes on sulking, telling his daughters 'come on children then and take it away and give it to the children.'

'Ahe sir! A person brings her food and a man is not well—it should not be given away, it should be kept for him to eat at another time.'

He says 'hm! Eh woman, does one argue with a father in this manner?'

They deceive him: 'oh no sir, I am not disputing anything sir!'

'Mistress, I do not feel well today, today is not a good day for me. I shall retire.'

'He! Look at that spying husband of mine, what an unpleasant character!'

The wife puts water before her lover as though he were her [male] husband. She has her penis in her bag—she takes it around with her. They carve a sweet potato into the shape of a circumcised penis. The woman–husband makes a hole through the sweet potato and then ties it with cord through it to her loins so that she is like a male. She washes herself with water and anoints herself with oil. Meanwhile the husband is eating his meal in the hut of his senior wife. [He says to her] 'with me you have never done me ill. My wife, that which I have seen, do you see it too?'

'No sir, but I have an idea about it. I am not sure of things sir! Eh sir! As you are a man, in a matter of this kind why do you not hear what she has to say to satisfy yourself in your mind?'

[He coughs]: 'all right, this death of mine they speak of, I will get to the bottom of it.'

The two women get up to lie on the ground because their movements on the bed make a noise. The wife of the man says 'friend, that spying husband of mine, he is nasty enough to try and trap people in a hut.' 'If he does he will die if he sees it. Madam do not weary yourself with thinking about women's affairs, you will see what happens. Let us do what we are going to do. Just stop talking about my husband.' She makes her keep quiet by shaking her head at her while she takes pleasure of her love.

The husband comes and crouches in the porch and he hears the sounds of them in the hut, as they say to each other in whispers 'o my darling, o my husband, o my lady.' He enters the hut and when they see him they rise from the ground. He seizes his wife. [He says to the other woman] 'o my friend you kill me. I thought you had come to my home in good-will, but it seems that it is my death you bring.' Then he calls his senior wife: 'Mistress come here and see what evil has befallen me—this woman I have taken hold of together with her companion . . .'

'Heyo! My husband, do you summon me to a woman's affair—your wives can be very malicious to me sir.'

'Eh woman! We share a home with you in double-talk. So you are all moved by wish for my death!'

'Hi! Leave off that talk with me—is it my fault that you went and entered the hut?'

MAN AND WOMAN

Men are seated and are thinking about women. One says to his friend 'women have no sense. A woman will marry a man and however handsome a man he may be she leaves him and goes after an ugly man, a squat little fellow; so a woman will go after him to sleep with him. Then when a case arises about it and it is taken to court the men at court say 'friend, look at that ill-looking fellow who has violated this man's wife, he is not worthy of her.' So a man says 'oh dear! That is what they say "women have no sense", for if a woman sees some ugly youth she wants to go after him.' That is why a man says about it to his companion 'if a man admonishes his wife and she replies "yes sir, I will not commit that bad fault again" her husband thinks that he had admonished her to good purpose, whereas the very next time she sees a man on the path and the man makes a suggestion to her she recalls what her husband told her and ignores it and lets another man have his way with her.'

It is by this sort of experience that men got to know about women's deceit. A woman likes to practise her deceit almost in the presence of her husband. She sits down saying 'oh I feel really ill today.' and she keeps on getting up at night to go into the bush [to the lavatory], whereas it is her lover she goes to visit, and she arranges her deceit with him, telling him to wait on the path to the ash-heap to await her there. This wife then gets up and goes along the path to the ash-heap and takes him and hides him nearby. Her lover knots his grass [for good fortune], and he goes after her and copulates with her right beside the ash-heap; and then she rises and returns home, and when she sees her husband she cries out 'm! M! Oh how ill I feel today!' Then she seats herself, but it is from her lover that she has come.

For a woman did precisely this in the past, so our fathers told us, saying 'there was once a man whose wife fell ill. She arose in the night saying that her stomach was badly upset and she asked her husband to light a handful of grass to escort her to the bush. The husband said to himself that it was all right, that since his wife was sick he would escort her to the bush. He and his wife went together. Now there was a hole they were digging behind the hut, and her lover had descended into it and had taken off his bark cloth and had laid it on the ground; and he had lain down on it to await her. She came along with her husband, and when her husband was standing to wait for her she went quickly and descended into the hole after her lover there. He then copulated with her; and she cried "m! O how sick I feel, how sick I feel." Her husband stood still holding up fire in his hand, for they were conversing; and she said to him "since you are very courageous, would a man go after your wife under your very eyes!" When they had finished copulating she arose and emerged at the edge of the hole, and the lover rose and took his bark cloth to wear it, to tuck it in thus. However, her husband was standing with a light in his hand thus while he helped her out of the hole. He asked her "eh! my wife, who is that man!" The man made a dash for it with all speed. The two men began to run and the husband chased the other. Then the flame in his hand went out. He jumped and came to earth thus, thinking that he had speared him; but he had not speared him, and the man escaped.

'He came and appeared after his wife; and he said to himself that he was ashamed because his wife had deceived him by copulating with a man right in the hole of a hut. He seized her to give her a good beating. She said to him "as you said how brave you were, that is why I summoned a man behind the hut for you."

She added "although you are so brave you did him no injury because of that argument you had with me, that argument made you fail (you told me before that if anyone came after me you could spear him, but you missed)." ' Therefore when a wife falls sick her husband likes to make sure what sickness it is. If he satisfies himself that she really is ill he says 'all right'; because a woman called her lover right in front of her husband behind a hut; so when a wife says she is sick her husband goes for just a little walk along the path and after dawdling there he returns slowly, and when he reaches his home he stops first behind the rubbish heap to listen for the speech of his wife in the home. If she is really sick he finds out that it is so, for women are deceivers, they deceive out of idleness, and out of lechery also. A woman seeks for some excuse to deceive her husband with it, and she hits on the idea of saying she is sick. Therefore Azande also say about women in a proverb *'akegobili'*,[1] for a woman says that she will do her husband no wrong whereas that is what she is always doing.

A TYPICAL CASE ABOUT ADULTERY

The prince comes and sits in his court beneath his court-hut and on his stool. A man whose wife has been abused by another stands before the prince to make his case to the prince for him to hear it: 'master, when a subject is in trouble, he who is a subject tells it to his master. Master, this man here has been turning my wife away from me. Since he began to go after her, which was at the end of the year, she has not listened to a word I told her any more. So I, your servant, considered the matter and I said to myself that this deceit my wife does to me, I will find it out right away. So I got up right early in the morning and told her that I was going to court, so she must cook a meal for me quickly so that I might go to court on the prince's affairs. My master, she prepared a meal for me like an honest woman and brought it to me; however, she had already prepared her lover's meal with eggs, whereas she cooked only oil for me, who am her husband. I said nothing, not a word, and I went on eating the porridge, and then I rose to go on my way. I continued on it till I reached the path to the

1. This is an archaic word the precise literal meaning of which is obscure. The sense however is clear: tricksters.

water, and I climbed that tall *banga* tree which is there and waited there. She arose before my eyes and took this porridge and put it in a water-pot and put a leaf over it. She then took this pot and placed it on her head. Master, she came right on before my eyes, and when she reached the path she left it beneath the *bakaikpo* tree and cut through the bush and took this porridge and placed it in the fork of a tree. All these things which she did, I witnessed all of them. She came and drew her water and then she returned, and when she reached the place where she had left the path with the porridge she drew water from the pot into a gourd and went and placed it by the side of the porridge, and then she went home. As soon as I knew that she had gone I at once climbed down the tree and went to the porridge. I then thought the matter over and I said to myself that I might leave it alone to lie in wait for him near it first; but then I thought inside myself that it would be better for me to take my porridge and eat it and then see what was about to happen. I took my porridge, master, and I went with it to my place in the tree. I ate it all up and then I waited. As I looked I saw them coming together. As I am your servant, I thought that since it was the days of European rule should I kill him I could then flee to the country of Wando. But my guardian angel told me not to do that; it were better that I seize them to get compensation in spears out of them. Master, when I climbed down the tree she already saw me as I was climbing down, for she was looking out for me. When she saw me she motioned him away with her hand to tell him to flee for her husband was coming, to flee quickly. He started off at full speed, master, and ran and ran till he disappeared. Then I came and seized the woman to give her a good thrashing; and then she told me that this man was the younger brother of so-and-so and that he had congress with her regularly. I told her that early next morning I would go with her to court so that she could tell the prince about her affair. If I had seen him in the act I would not have spared him, I would have paid no attention to the word of the Europeans and killed him in truth.'

The prince says 'young man, come and speak about this affair, how it came about that you have led the wife of this man away from him.' He comes before the prince and he says to him 'master, it seems that that hatred your subjects have for me in your domain explains the lie this man has told you. If it were true that he really saw me with his wife why did he not at once seize me?' When the case stood thus that elder [the husband] rises and says to the prince thus: 'master, this man, the woman's speech accuses him, you summon the woman herself, let her come and say on her part how she began it.' The prince says 'all right, let her come and say her part.' She comes before the prince and says to the prince 'yes, master, that man there, he denies it vainly, for it was he who sent his sister after me, telling her to say to me that he wanted me to be with him. So I said to myself that since it was he who had started the affair with me I would do what he wanted; for he told me that if I refused him he would kill me with sorcery and burn the dung of wagtails with tobacco towards me so that I would become barren and not take another husband. That is why I consented to his proposal, for it is an old affair and I have been with him now for several months.' The elders say to her 'woman, your evidence is finished. It is you who make fun of us elders. Today we will give you something to think about.' The prince then says to the adulterer 'why did you lie to me in the first place, saying that you did not go after this woman.' He replies to the prince 'master, it was the speech of terror of men, that is why I told a lie about it.' The prince asks him, saying 'did you know the wife of this man carnally?' He replies to the prince 'yes, master, when I desired her she said she loved me very much, and that is why I sent a message to her.' The case then goes against him at once, and the prince says to him 'you pay him twenty spears, and you will pay another five because you lied to me.' The husband now comes and sits before the prince and wipes the ground and lies prostrate before the prince, and he gathers grass and dry leaves before the prince, and then he rises and goes to seat himself in his place. Then the pages hold on to the wife and give a hoe to her and another to the man and put them to work in the prince's court, to hoe it quite clean. They hoe it till evening falls and they have completed the task, and then they allow them to depart. The adulterer collects the first five spears of his fine and places them before the prince. The prince gives them to one of his elders and tells him to follow up the case until all the compensation has been paid and he brings it to him here. When all the compensation has been paid the husband of the woman sets aside for this elder some five spears for the trouble he has taken, as messenger, with this adulterer. Then all is from that moment finished between them.

ADULTERY

This is about how a husband meets on the path that man who has had relations with his wife. When he sees the adulterer ahead he has already made ready his place at the side of the path to lie in wait for him to spear him. The adulterer comes on and when he is about to pass the husband stands up and spears him. The spear pierces him through '*puu*', and that man falls to the ground with a cry of dismay '*wuwo*' on his lips. He cries out, saying, 'Alas man you did not ask me, when I could have explained things to you; you came to kill me. I have many kinsmen and they would have paid compensation for me so that I might have survived. O sir, what a wicked man you are!'

The husband drags his body a long way till he is deep in the bush nearby the burrow which he saw before and he pushes him into it and places grass over his head carefully. He then take a little of his blood and tastes it [to keep his strength which would otherwise depart from him]; for if he did not do so he might not reach his home, for a man's blood is a terrible thing. He twines *bingba* grass and binds it round his wrist, for it is the custom that when a man kills another he binds *bingba* grass round his wrist. If you see this grass round a man's wrist it means that he has killed a man. Those elders of [King] Gbudwe's time liked killing people.

A MAN AND A WOMAN: AN ADULTERY CASE

That woman who wishes to speak straight to a man, she says to him, 'o man why are you denying since you never ceased persisting after me. People, since you sit here, be quiet and let me tell my affair which I have come to tell about this man.'

[The man]: 'all right I am silent, all right I am silent.'

[The prince]: 'then what are you talking about? Be quiet.'

[The woman]: 'eh man, since you deny that you had intercourse with me, did you not say that I should not continue in marriage with my husband, you were going to marry me? I say to you "eh when you made love to me you said that I should leave my husband to go and marry you."'

Lovers and Adulterers

[The father of the adulterer]: 'eh woman, eh woman, prince I have got something to say.'

[The father's blood-brother]: 'ye! What has it got to do with you? It has nothing whatever to do with you my blood-brother.'

[The woman]: 'don't you butt into our affairs. Be silent with yours over there sir.' [To the man]: 'do you say that you did not sleep with me in a hut, that I slept by myself just like a widow?'

[The prince]: 'so, you would marry for what? If you cook a meal for a man and the man eats it till he is replete, then desire for a woman comes over him all the time; a hunger for making love to a woman takes hold of him, it takes hold of a man. Why do you say that you did not enter her hut, after her into a hut in her home?' She yodels the prince '*tai yai yai*.'

[An old elder]: 'prince do we not talk childish talk round here. . . . I have not before seen anything like what goes on here. I say this to you prince because you are the son of my master.'

[The man]: 'those people, all of them, they dislike me.'

[The old elder]: 'why do they dislike you?'

[The man]: 'sir, sure they dislike me because if there were anyone who bore me the slightest good will he would speak well of me to the prince. They don't let me have my say and they spoil my case. Who heard my side of the case since the woman has been giving hers now? And when I thought to have my say the prince would not listen to my speech.'

[The prince]: 'all right have your say.'

[The man]: 'this woman whom you see sir, this woman whom you see, she is a bad woman. If I went into a hut in her home. . . . I say that if I came out of the doorway one of the other wives would have seized me, saying "has he finished intercourse with her [the wives are sex-starved]?" If I had been into the hut in the homestead there I would have put all my things in order. Why should I just stand by the door of the hut like a witch-doctor?[1] I would stand in the doorway like a witch-doctor while he went to another hut to sleep there. There are others there to whose huts he goes; does one sleep with a stone? Does one sleep with a stone?'

The prince [to the woman's husband]: 'let her go as she is crying for you. Go away with her and settle her there. You admonish her and tell her not to show enmity to your wives. That

1. This is what witch-doctors often do during their dances.

sort of thing is not very nice in a home. She is much desirous of men. But you had better take some virility medicine for her.'

Those present laugh and say: 'o prince do you not settle cases right away here!'

[An old man]: 'so! My blood-brother so! Come to me, I have *gagaga* medicine and I will mash it up for you with eleusine malt, and you will absorb it into your body. Your spear will then be straight [your penis will be erect]—[the people laugh]—Don't think I do not have this medicine my blood-brother. A man becomes impotent and I mash it for him and he is like a drumstick [his penis is erect]—[they laugh].'

[The prince]: 'take her away and return with her.' [To the woman]: 'do not show enmity to his wives.'

[The husband]: '*ai* my master, a man does not sit with a fire of *dakpa* wood—what shall I do?'

[The woman]: 'he is wasting his time. Why did you marry me in the first place? If you go far away I will go with you. You eat something there and you will find me when you come back. Don't think I am like those other women you have married. I reprove my husband about madness; they will bury us together, I with that husband of mine.'

[The husband]: 'o mistress, that habit of yours is not good, lady.'

[The wife]: '*he!* And what is this habit of mine? You tell it, I swear by my mother's head! Man! Do I steal things? Am I mean? Since I married you have I gone after other men? I get up early in the morning and sweep the whole place clean and I kindle my husband's fire!'

[The husband]: 'hm! *Oho* lady, *eh* do you think I have told all? Does one tell everything?'

[The wife]: 'hm! Who tears the mouth of my entrails [who is saying bad things about me]?'

[The husband]: '*ehe* people, you see the manner of her affairs!'

[The wife]: 'prince, those habits he has seen, let him relate them all.'

[The husband]: 'hm! You there, are you not elders? If one told everything one would have to speak about witchcraft.'

[The wife]: '*he!* You are saying that I bewitch you sir?'

[The husband's father]: 'no no lady, he did not mean that lady, he did not mean that, that you bewitch him.'

[The prince]: 'that person with whom this affair began, this affair began. . . . What is it all about?'

[An old elder]: 'yes prince, you speak the truth, let us hear it from their mouths.'

[The husband's father]: '*he yo!* An elder passes by a snail, a child takes it. Yes prince their affair is like the inside of a snake [they talk so that no one can understand them].'

[The prince]: 'as they talk thus how will they get things straightened out?'

[The woman]: 'everything I have done—these men who speak against me, they have all partaken of food prepared by me. I will not show my hand to my neighbours again [I won't prepare any more food for them].'

[The prince]: 'you are a stupid woman. All of you go away. I have had enough of it.'

MUTILATION

In the past, when a man had relations with the wife of another the case was brought before Gbudwe. He whom Gbudwe did not wish to die, he summoned some three of his senior men and told them to go and mutilate that man on account of the wife of so-and-so. However, when they went, they must not kill him, they must just mutilate him. They went on their way and saw him seated. They had previously arranged a plot among themselves, which was 'since he has a knife, you go as though you were just passing him and then fall on him suddenly.' Having made this plan between them, they went on their way and when they approached him the man who was to seize him went as though he was passing him by; then all of a sudden he grappled with him and held him firmly; and he cried out, saying 'you there! I have the man. Oh you there! To my assistance. I have the man, come and join me with the man.' The others began to seize him and they bound him tightly, twisting his arms behind his back and binding them tightly, and binding his legs also. Then they took a razor, a very sharp one. They took hold of one of his hands and bent it backwards, and as they cut it with the knife it broke [at the joint]. Then they severed the skin at the back of the wrist. When that was finished, they did the same with the other hand; and then they sliced off his genitals, and then they cut off his upper lip and both his ears.

THE MUTILATION OF GBITARANGBA[1]

I arose—we were living on the Yubo river at the time—I arose and took my belt of metal beads and tied it round my waist. So, I arose and went on my way to the home of my father's elder brother. A woman met me on the path and said to me that I should give her the metal beads. The husband of her younger sister then met me on the path and asked me 'what were you talking about with her?' And then he seized me and they bound me with cord. My kinsmen, they began to ransom me, to pay their spears to so many, so let them leave me alone as they were paying spears thus, let them not mutilate me. But they said no, they were going to mutilate him. So they mutilated me; and they returned all their spears to my kinsmen. So it was, and then came the European who killed Gbudwe and he sent a messenger after the man who had mutilated me, but he had left his home and fled from the command of the European.[2]

VENGEANCE

That debt Azande exacted in the past was this: if a man gave spears to the kin of a woman and then that woman kept on running away to her parents and there had relations with many men, then if her husband was enraged by her behaviour he killed her. When her relatives heard about it they refused to return his marriage-spears. That was the custom of the Azande in the past. But today if things are like that her husband makes a case against her father.

Another debt is this: if a man in the past killed one of your kinsmen you would take your spear and go and slay one of his clan to make things even. And if a man killed another with witch-

1. I took down this account of what happened to him from Gbitarangba himself. He received the full ghastly punishment for adultery, including emasculation and the loss of both hands.
2. Therefore this event took place round about 1904.

craft and the dead man's kin consulted the poison oracle and the oracle said that that man was responsible for the death, then the kin went and slew him to even things.

That man who committed adultery with the wives of others in the past and it became known; if they did not wish to kill him, Gbudwe would order him to pay twenty spears and his wife also, since his wife played her part in the adultery. But if they wished to kill the man they did so.

A SCANDAL

One afternoon Kamunga's sister came to visit him. She was in a bad temper with her husband, a member of the Belanda people by birth. Her chief complaint against her husband was that he had said that Kamunga had sexual relations with her. Kamunga was grieved and resentful at this suggestion, and so he kept his sister with him. Nyabani (a neighbour) said that evening that the sister had better sleep in her hut and not in Kamunga's, since such an insinuation had been made; and so it was arranged.

Some days later the husband arrived to ask his wife to return. Kamunga threw in his face this disgraceful scandal, but he denied all knowledge of it. Talk went on for two or three days longer. Kamunga was only about fifteen years of age and his brother-in-law was a fully grown man; but it was Kamunga who was in the dominant position and his grown-up brother-in-law had to humble himself. The husband wanted to start for home that same afternoon with his wife. Kamunga agreed to let her go but insisted on their departure being delayed till next day. He insisted on this as a final show of authority. His brother-in-law wiped the ground with deference such as is shown to princes and thanked Kamunga, exclaiming '*ako gbia*,' ('thank you master').

MEN CONVERSE ON A PATH

Kisanga went out walking one morning and on reaching the path he met some men. One of them asked me [Kisanga] where I was going to. I replied to him 'you see me my friend on my way to my mother-in-law's. You ask me to what purpose?'

[The man]: 'hm! I did not know you were married.'

[Kisanga]: 'my friend, why do you question me about it?'

[The man]: 'I just ask you sir as a man asks a friend whom he meets on the path.'

[Kisanga]: 'you go on with your bad habits. I have heard about you, that you have been to speak ill of me to my mother-in-law.'

[The man]: '*ye!* Eh man! Those men who copulate with your wife, I am not among them. It is you and your younger brothers who are giving my wife a bad reputation.'

[Kisanga]: 'all right sir, if you say you know of something between me and your wife we will have it out with you in court.'

[The man]: 'hm! Those wives who have left me, it is you and your younger brothers who have spoilt them. Eh sir, the British are here and so is Prince Gangura, so we will make a case between us before the British.'

[Kisanga]: 'sir, I did not start this talk about you myself; it was my mother-in-law who said that you people came to my home after my wife. So I said that if I saw the fellow I would spear him with my spear. As you and your fathers have married your own women why do you dispute with me about my single wife?'

[The man]: 'o master, if I attack a man at your in-laws the British will seize me and put me in prison.'

[Kisanga]: 'eh man! That business of your copulating with my wife, the British will say that you have wantonly had congress with my wife.'

[The man]: 'o man!' [followed by an untranslatable curse].

[Kisanga]: 'so fellow you wantonly insult me.'

[The man]: 'hm! Fellow how does one insult one's slave?'

[Another elder tries to make peace between them].

[The second man]: '*ye!* My son eh! By the limb of my father you are talking like children. My children, stop all this nonsense.'

[The first man]: 'master, don't try to calm me, you calm Kisanga.'

[Kisanga]: 'ai my master! Woman-talk is no good.'

[The second man]: 'eh my son! You know it just as I do. You say it is woman-talk. Well, you go home my son, you go home.'

[Kisanga]: 'you are right, you are right about your wife. That elder brother of yours who died, people treated him ill about his wife. He died as a result of putting *moti* medicine on his wife, that powerful medicine. All this led to his death to no purpose. Eh my father! You have spoken well sir! They might kill me on account of my wife. Their father has consulted the oracle about me for his sons, asking whether they should spear me with their spears sir; for I have no father, my father is already dead who might have consulted the poison oracle on my behalf. My father is no longer here. I shall not do anything wantonly that people might stab my belly with knives.'

[the second man]: 'right my son, since your father is dead you listen to what your older friend says. I know what your father used to say. Don't get yourself killed for a woman, for woman-trouble began long ago.'

BAD HABITS OF MEN

Among the Azande there are many with bad habits. You set out with a man of bad habits, and although some trouble falls on you, such as sickness, he will leave you alone and wander off somewhere else. Such a one says he is not going to inform your relatives about your trouble lest they put the blame on him. And if he is going along with you and men attack you he keeps well away from where the men are beating you; he wanders away from you and you do not see him. However, if on some other day you see him he makes some crafty excuse, such as saying 'the men gave me a bad time of it, that is why I ran away, it was to escape death at their hands.' If he is your companion when people seize you on account of a beer-debt,[1] although he has the wherewithal to pay it he will not give it to you to save you from the people. Even though you both drank the beer together he will not ransom you [he will not even pay his share] but will wait for you to think up some story to tell it to the owner of the beer. If the owner is a good man he will leave you alone and tell you to go and find some money and bring it to him right away. But if he is a bad man he will strip you of everything you possess, leaving you without a thing. But if you have a blood-brother nearby who will help you you will leave that man and fetch him. Even though your companion hears tales about you he does not let you know but keeps them from you. He himself is a tale-teller, and he hopes you will suffer misfortune.

1. The beer is put out for sale and you drink it and then say that you will pay for it later as you have no money now.

Part II
MODERN TIMES

Preface

As I explained at the beginning of the book, the texts in Part II were written for me by either Mr. Mambia or Mr. Beda, both students in the University of Khartoum before the troubles began and caused them to vacate that university; Mr. Mambia going to the Congo and Mr. Beda first to the Congo and then to Nigeria. They were written in Zande with English translations. All I have done is to make sure that the English version corresponds faithfully to the Zande version.

The tenses vary according to whether these two young men were writing about past events or what older persons told them was past custom. Here, in the matters dealt with, what is recorded would, in my experience, be true of the Azande of some forty years ago (when I was last in their country); though there is sometimes, as might be expected, a difference of perspective or emphasis. A number of these are conversation pieces, a genre which I found most useful when among the Azande of the Sudan between the years 1926 and 1930, both for learning the idiomatic language and for conveying its flavour in translation to students and others. They are, of course, imaginary conversations, but they are the kind of conversations which take place daily, just as among ourselves the conversations in a good work of fiction tell us the thoughts and feelings and manners of real people.

The pieces often presented formidable difficulties in translation. Although these pieces were written many years after I began my research in Zandeland they reflect the same attitudes and expression of them as were then current and are set forth in the texts recorded in Part I of this volume. In particular—and this is what, besides their idiomatic character, makes them so difficult to render into English—there is always the tendency, as I have said before, in Zande conversation to use circumlocutory or double-talk language—what the Azande call *sanza*—in which it is necessary to catch the notes of understatement, innuendo, teasing, irony, raillery, sarcasm or just plain malice. And beneath the badinage

141

and bickering and gossiping there is, whether expressed or not, the same old underlying, but near-surface, presence of witchcraft hovering around.

Much has changed among the Azande since 1930, much that I have never seen myself: towns, shops, industry, controlled farming and cash crops, a money economy, markets, the spread of Christianity, cotton clothes, alcoholic spirits, prostitution, and other innovations, introduced, directly or indirectly, and usually, in the first instance at any rate, imposed by the British. However, many habits of thought and feeling, judged by these texts, seem to have changed little, possibly only on the surface; but without having had the chance to visit the country since 1930 I cannot express a definite opinion on how deep the changes have been and whether they are widespread or more or less restricted in their full impact to the sophisticated town-dweller. I have to guess from the texts and from what I have learnt from Dr. Reining's *The Zande Scheme* (1966). Nor can I, or anybody else at present, say what has happened since the Sudan Government has waged a repressive campaign over the last few years against the Southern Sudanese, including the Azande.

I should perhaps add, since the topic of this book is man and woman, that although today women may assert themselves more than they used to, and be rather more tart, the relationship between the sexes does not seem to be fundamentally different to what it was in my day and, so Azande told me, has always been.

It has also to be pointed out that, as might be presumed, these texts in Part II are stylistically different from those in Part I. The earlier ones were dictated, or at any rate related, by Azande unacquainted with writing; these later ones were written by young men with a literary background sufficient to have taken them to the University of Khartoum. There is no need for me to enter here into a discussion of what these differences are in the vernacular but it will be evident that they appear also in the English translations, for I have left the translations made by my two friends with the minimum interference (dictionaries are not always a sure guide to sense); so that the English texts in the two sections of the book are for the most part by different hands.

Husbands and Wives
and Lovers and Families

When a man married many wives and had many children—boys and girls—the bridewealth of the girls was divided among the boys. A boy did not have the use of his full sister's bridewealth, only that of a half-sister [a sister by a different mother].

The father took the bridewealth of the eldest daughter. Then he divided up the bridewealth of the others among his sons. The children's ages were carefully noted, and it was known which child was born first even when two wives might be delivered on the same day. A boy got the bridewealth of a girl younger than he (the last son might not get any bridewealth but when he grew up his father and uncles would give him spears for marriage). So when a boy was still small he already knew from which of his sisters he would receive her bridewealth.

If there were many more daughters than sons the father could take the bridewealth of two or three of them. A good and generous father would give some bridewealth also to sons of his elder and younger brothers. If there were more boys than girls those who had no younger sisters, after their father and elder brothers were satisfied, might go without bridewealth.

A young man used his sister's bridewealth for his own marriage. So those without sisters would visit their paternal and maternal uncles that they might give them spears to marry with. If the father was alive he would offer such a son some ten spears and say 'go to your fathers [uncles] and grandfathers that they may give you spears for a wife.'

When a man died the relatives of his wife returned her bridewealth to his relatives after the period of mourning. All the spears were returned. The father of the dead man or one of his brothers went to make a case about these spears if the widow did not marry one of her dead husband's kinsmen. In most cases the widow married one of her dead husband's brothers, so the bridewealth was not returned. When a wife died her bridewealth was kept by her relatives.[1]

When the brother of a woman died his elder brother would take over the bridewealth of the dead man's sister. When a woman's brothers all died and there was nobody to look after her, especially if she was ill-treated by her husband, one of her young relatives would take up her case, deal with those hurting her, and take her to his home. He might travel to a distant court for this purpose. When she was married he took her bridewealth. So a man fond of litigation and successful in it might get hold of other bridewealth [than that of his sister], bridewealth of female relatives who were suffering from their husbands and had no brothers to protect them.

A man who had only one wife and many sons and daughters also divided up the bridewealth like a man with many wives. He took for himself the bridewealth of the eldest daughter and the rest went to his sons.

When husbands died and their widows married their younger brothers or kinsmen or even their senior sons, the sons whose fathers had died knew the bridewealth of which sisters they were to take.

When the husband of a woman died she could marry a younger brother or a senior son of her husband. Elders used to marry young girls, so on the death of an elder these girls could marry his senior sons (my grandfather has five wives but there is only one of them he himself married, the other four are widows of his father and were taken by him when his father died. Two other such widows of his elder brother died in my grandfather's home years ago).

HUSBAND AND WIFE (ABOUT MEAT)

Husband: 'ee child, madam, I have not eaten at your hands since early morning?'

1. This account is an over-simplification of what happened when a wife or husband died. Whether the bridewealth, or some of it, was returned depended on such considerations as the number and sex of the children born in the union, whether the widow was remarried to a kinsman of her dead husband, and whether a widower was given another spouse in the place of his dead wife.

Wife: 'hii, where will I find meat to make porridge to go with it, sir? There is no early morning now but that other men take their nets and go hunting. If you just sit like me who am a woman, will meat get up in the bush and come to you on its feet?'

Husband: 'o my sister, madam, I always used to kill animals before and you prepared their flesh [cut them up for cooking] just like the wives of those who kill them now; hee, can you deny it? Look you, it is the Azande who have spoilt my hunting with their witchcraft. This year I have carried my hunting net to no purpose, without even taking the foreleg of a [small] grey duiker. What can I do, madam? Ha! Just cook my groundnuts for me for which I hoe their plot; I don't hoe a plot for meat.'

Wife: 'is it just the old animals you used to kill when Gbudwe was reigning, is it those you are boasting about? Shall we eat the meat of those today? I suppose that when a man does not kill for a long time he makes *bingia* medicine or else calls on a magician to come and put medicine on his [hunting] net? All right, let us just sit and eat our manioc leaves.'

Husband: 'who told you it is good to call medicine into the home? Didn't Mbaraza call it here, and only his senior wife suffered, as she was the one who spoilt his chances of killing animals, saying why should he give some of the meat to the other wives when he killed an animal? He should give her alone the entire carcase. . . .'

Wife: 'do you think that if you bring *bagbuduma* medicine today I will die and people will say it was his wife who spoilt his hunting?'

Husband: 'did I say to you now it is you who are bewitching my hunting? You are harping so much on my case, though this year all other wives have been catching fish, have you looked there [thought of that]? It is only some time ago that you went fishing once; have you ever looked to the river since?'

Wife: 'hii, I have too many little jobs to do or I would also go to catch my fish, and. . . .'

Husband: 'those catching fish now, haven't they got many little jobs? Just say about it that you just don't want to catch fish for me to eat.'

Wife: 'why should I refuse to fish for you, since when you kill an animal it belongs to me? As you have not killed any these days my brother, have I seen the heads of anybody's eleusine sir? As they are killing them this year they don't cast a look at me. My friends for whom I used to cut off huge pieces of meat, when their husbands kill, they look up at the sky beside it [when I am present]. Oh these Azande ooo hee!'

Husband: 'did they (not) tell you that there is nothing Azande are so mean about as meat? When a Zande sees his meat he refuses to recognize anybody. When he has finished it he may then talk with the rest of us.'

Wife: 'and when they see yours they want to kill you because of it, as they did with Doka's wife a while ago about a waterbuck, and the woman only just escaped the grave.'

Husband: 'anyhow she is very mean. When a big animal like that dies you should cut the ribs for your women friends.'

Wife: 'so you have started that, and when it gets around they will say it was you who bewitched her, as people are not particular what they say these days. All right!'

HUSBAND AND WIFE (ABOUT HUTS)

Wife: 'oh! Zaza has built a big kitchen-hut for his wife, such a big hut, just like the kitchen-hut you built for me in our old home.'

Husband: 'it is that it is you who are too lazy to cut grass [for thatching] this year or I would have built another one for you. You will just have to see it in other people's homes.'

Wife: 'have you started cutting down the supports [poles] that I should kill myself by cutting grass? Didn't you do the same thing once before and my loads of grass just rotted? You are also too lazy to build a hut.'

Husband: 'who has been building to shelter you? Name him, ee madam, name him if you please! Is it not I who have been building big huts for you?'

Wife: 'you build all right. Those ugly little huts I see in people's homes are never found here in yours, but it is only that you build the granary very high! [Probably sarcasm.]'

Husband: 'when you leave me and marry another man rain will beat down on you outside until your eyes are red, by my father's limb!'

Wife: 'hueee [a laugh], and then why not return to you? A woman is never ashamed to return to her old home [husband]. Hiii, who can sleep in a dilapidated hut?'

Husbands and Wives and Lovers and Families

HUSBAND AND WIFE (ABOUT CULTIVATING)

Wife: 'ee man! As everybody has started his groundnuts cultivation, what shall we do this year? I have waited long enough for you to show me a plot so that I may go and begin scratching the ground there, but what is happening? Say, won't we eat this year?'

Husband: 'let people cultivate their groundnuts; have I eaten before in their homes?'

Wife: '*ai!* That is the kind of talk one indulges in while the season for things passes. I don't like planting groundnuts late. It is better to go to the bush [start cultivating] along with other people. If I lack groundnuts who will give them to me, since my mother is dead? And relatives are not kind when it comes to their possessions.'

Husband: 'have you ever lacked groundnuts before that you should lack them this year?'

Wife: 'I am speaking because we have the work of the [mortuary] feast hanging over us. It is not good for a feast to remain over people's heads. People have all lamented for their dead, and dances have been held in everybody's homes except ours, as if we don't cultivate. That sort of thing makes an elder appear small in the eyes of others. Your sons are shaving already, and you act like a child?'

A SECOND WIFE

Man: 'oh, my sister, I have seen an unmarried woman in this neighbourhood, you go and ask her hand for me.'

His wife: 'you go and marry your woman. I wouldn't marry a woman for you again. So! Is it not I who persuaded a woman for you before and you nearly killed me for her sake? And as for my hut, I never saw your footprints in its doorway. Can I myself again go to bring death on my head?'

Man: 'that sounds like jealousy. My father had many wives and his homestead spread as far as that stream over there. It is only I who have married only you, and you have refused to let me have another wife.'

His wife: 'it isn't me, it is you who have spoilt your chances of a second wife. And if your father married other wives and then treated his first wife like dirt would he have had many?'

Man: 'it is like this my sister, when you are sick my strength is exhausted from drawing water and collecting firewood. It is better that you should be two so when one is sick the other can help her, that is why I am saying this.'

His wife: 'you met this woman of yours a long time ago and you became her lover and you have been doing all sorts of things with her, did you think I didn't know about it? Is it today that you confess about her to me? When you marry her I shall go to my home. You nearly killed me before for the sake of a thief.'

Man: 'look here child, madam, I didn't know her before. It was only yesterday that I heard about her from her younger sister, Ngbaime's wife, that her [husband's] marriage-spears have been returned. That is why I went to have a look at her today.'

His wife: 'ah! Just collect your spears, sir, and go and marry your wife with them. Don't bother me any more. Let her come so that I may sometimes leave you [with her] to go to my home to regain my strength.'

Man: '*ai*, if you are so irritable about it I won't go. I thought I would come to speak to you about it first so that you might go and have a friendly talk with her, and if you should hear something [favourable] about it, then we would go with spears [bridewealth].'

His wife: 'am I your mother to ask the hands of women for you? That will never happen to me my brother. If you marry another wife you won't see me making war on her unless out of malice she starts trouble with me. Our clan don't know the hating of co-wives. Let her come to do for you the things I don't do, so that I may learn them.'

Man: 'you see, it is not like that at all, child, madam. It is because I thought it good to have two wives in the home. Now if I were to go out and your children to disperse also to their homes to whom would you talk?'

His wife: 'you go then to marry a woman so that she may help me in wearying myself for you [to feed you] and kindling [fire] for you. I am exhausted, I have become thin on the hearth [from too much cooking]. If she comes I shall be able to regain my health a little.'

Man: 'won't you accompany me tomorrow?'

His wife: 'if you gather your spears together we will go, or you will say I have been spoiling every plan of yours about women. But let me warn you beforehand that if you treat me like dirt because you have married a young blooming one I will quietly collect my children and return to my people [home]. Hear it well and get it into your head, that is all.'

Man: 'she is not so young as you make her out to be child, madam.'

HUSBANDS AND WIVES

A: 'friend, you are coming from the court, what's going on there?

B: 'nothing, only that Makpiri collected the marriage-spears of his wife today.'

C: 'eee, friend, although he treated her so well?'

B: 'do you say this about women? Although you do all sorts of things for a woman, kill animals for her, hoe for her till her granaries are full, the day she has in mind her departure she will never think about these things. She sits and eats up all these things and wipes her mouth afterwards and then jumps from you and lands as far as right over there.'

A: 'sir, do you suppose women to be your comrades? These women you see are tricksters. Even if a woman is so kind to you as to take something from a dog and put it away high up you will understand by that that she has a lover who eats the best [the head] of your things.'

B: 'people do not marry thinking it is thus [that wives are faithful]; it seems that it [marriage] began long ago with our forefathers to come down to us.'

C: 'you are telling the very truth. There is a type of woman who, although she has bad habits, yet she fears very much to let her husband go hungry. You kill an animal for her and you think that its flesh is all finished, and then there comes a day when you have forgotten all about it and she will bring out for you what she has put on one side; and then you will be perplexed about women.'

A: 'there are some who combine both laziness and stinginess so that you do not know which is the greater of the two. I married a woman and hoed a cultivation for her; but I never knew what she did with that eleusine, by my father's thigh! If she brewed the first of it and I invited people for it I would not see the elders' one big full pot.'[1]

B: 'women have different characters. There are some who eat meat while it is still being cooked just as there are men who say to a woman "bring the pot here so that I may cut you some meat into it." '[2]

C: 'sir, I will not find a wife again like my wife who died. I tell you the woman excelled in making beer. The woman would bring out the bowl filled to the brim with porridge. Sir, nobody could be hungry in my home . . .'

B: 'I interrupt you sir to tell you that good habits do not last. Sir, there is a type of poisonous woman who insults chicken and insults dogs. The worst of it is when she hears a rumour that you intend to marry a second wife. She will spend three days in her home without you as much as smelling her food.'

A: 'Although the woman in my home has bad habits she doesn't refuse me food. When my relatives come she does not say I should be present first, but she cooks something to quiet their hunger. If there happens to be beer I will return and meet them on their way staggering from the beer.'

C: 'sir, it is a good-mannered woman who does so, for relatives say "he is a very generous man, he is an elder's son," and not without cause, because when they come to your home they do not suffer hunger.'

A: 'since you don't cook porridge, if you have a nasty woman in your home, then your relatives will be spoiling your name.'

B: 'you sir e, did not a bad woman spoil our elder brother's home, the one who is our master? He does not bury his kin, who would cook for the people?'[3]

WIVES AND HUSBANDS (TWO WOMEN CONVERSE)

A: 'o child are you nowadays in the home? What is going on there? Is the elder [master of the home] present?'

1. The sense here is that she did not brew a special pot of beer for her husband to drink with his special friends apart from other guests.
2. So that the husband will know when the meat is served to him whether his wife has taken some of it for herself. This is regarded as very mean behaviour. A generous man gives all the meat to his wife to be used as she thinks fit.
3. Mortuary ceremonies require the preparation of food for the guests.

B: 'madam o, the man is in his home. As I went to my parents, I have only just got back. The master of the home said I had spent too long there and all the work of the home had gone bad. I said to him "sir o, I was visiting my withered mother." '

A: 'this habit of men, do they mean that a person should not go to visit her mother? Although my husband has bad habits he doesn't get angry when I spend many days with my parents because he knows that the day I return from there he will smile happily.'

B: 'o madam, I have returned with things for him in vain. The first time I went I returned with a pot of beer for him, and my mother ground flour and took a fowl together with dried meat and termite-oil, and accompanied me with these things, and he ate everything. This time also I returned with things for him.'

A: 'look you, a man doesn't want his wife to be far from him.'

B: 'are there not others at home madam, does he lack women?'

A: 'look you, although a man has many wives, there is only one of them who takes care of him. Women, as you see, are too stingy with their husbands. When a woman finds her meat she consumes it without her husband knowing. When hunger overcomes the man the woman is replete. Then with another woman, although something is very small she cooks this thing, and when the man comes to pass by she beckons him and puts this thing before him and it makes him strong. When he sees this, the man's eyes stay with you. When you go somewhere he looks towards the path [for your return], as though his other wives were not present.'

B: 'is that not the reason why his wives would like to kill me? There is nothing, however small, I would eat without him. The man is so generous to me that they wish to kill me. The reason for hating me is only this matter which you see.'

A: 'your husband has good manners. He does not beat you often. The man in whose home I am, oh, you see me with trouble.'

B: 'yes, he does not beat us often. He does not follow [spy on] us either. He doesn't give us meat to ask about it again, even though we cook for him only manioc leaves.'

A: 'my husband too, he doesn't share some people's great desire for food. He eats only a bit and leaves it. Only his habit of fighting and dislike of his wife talking to another man. . . .'

B: 'that is the same with all men. What man can bear to see his wife talking with other men without getting angry?'

A: 'as for mine [husband], it is too much. Did he not one day want to beat the son of my mother's husband for annoying me [paying attention to me]? If he caught his wife with a man he would kill her if the man escaped him.'

B: 'my last husband whom I left, I left him because of his sulking about his things. The man was like fire with me about his groundnuts. He hated my giving food to my friends. He was worst when he killed an animal for then he would tell me to cook for him only by night. He liked eating inside his hut. I said [to myself] "*ai*, my mother's child o, this won't happen to me." I left him with his stinginess.'

A: 'whose food is to be eaten by a man alone by himself? I like to cook food in plenty and bring it out in a bowl to the brim so that my husband may eat with his friends and they praise his name for it. I cannot marry a mean man. Food does not wail for a person, only those friends who when you die come to chase the flies away from your corpse.'

B: 'that is the thing girl. This husband of mine [who is generous] will divorce me before I go and get caught up with another [whose character and whims I do not know].'

A COURT CASE

Bangunza was a subject of Prince Rikita and he married a wife fron Rikita's province. They lived together for a long time and had two children, a daughter and a son. Bangunza was not a good husband, so his wife left him for her kin when she could not stand him any longer. When he had followed her to their home and failed to bring her back he summoned her and her brother to appear before Rikita's elders at court.

Bangunza: 'sirs, I can't imagine what I have done that has provoked my wife to leave me. My masters, I have done many things for that woman you see before you, but in vain. I leave it to you to question and get out of her the reason she has deserted the home of her children's father to wander about like a girl.'

The elders: 'wife of Bangunza, you have heard what he said. What is the situation?'

Bangunza's wife: 'sirs, that man you see before you, don't be deceived by his appearance. He is terrible to live with. I have tried to forbear in vain. He cut meat for me into the cooking pot. He has eaten up everything from me. He has. . . .'

Bangunza: 'my masters, I do what elders in my position do. Sirs, if an elder kills meat and brings it home from the bush and calls for his wife to bring the cooking pot so that we may cut up the meat into it, is that a bad thing?'

The elders 'it isn't at all Bangunza.'

Bangunza: 'you woman who has been humiliating me for so long, we shall argue a lot today. My masters, I have not eaten anything from her. If a wife cooks meat and leaves it on the fire to go and fetch water at the stream, and if the broth smells good so that the man takes out a bit, puts it on a leaf and eats it while waiting for his woman with water, is that a bad thing?'

The elders: 'Bangunza there is not the slightest thing bad in that. It is the same for all.'

Bangunza: 'you woman with those red eyes of yours, I shall return with you today. Sirs, if a wife roasts shelled groundnuts and goes to fetch firewood while they are left to cool and you happen to come in the manner of elders and take a handful of them to throw into your mouth one by one on your way to cut your rope [bast] have you wronged the woman?'

The elders: 'not the slightest bit Bangunza.'

Bangunza: 'do you hear that mistress! You of the court, if you and your wife catch a lot of termites and she winnows [cleans] them and you weave a basket for storing them over the fireplace in the sleeping hut and when the woman is absent you make a hole at the base of the basket and cause some of the termites to pour into an elder's straw hat through the hole and chew them while walking round your cultivations is that theft?'

The elders: 'Bangunza, can a man steal his own property?'

Bangunza: 'o my masters, I am sick of being degraded by this woman you see before you.' [To his wife]: 'those eyes of yours, today the case between you and me will be properly settled.' [To the elders]: 'if a woman goes to visit her relatives and when you, an elder, are hungry and climb into the granary and take out groundnuts and eleusine to give to somebody else to prepare food for you and save you from hunger, have you finished the woman's things by doing that?'

The elders: 'Bangunza, did your wife leave you because of these things you have been telling us?'

Bangunza: 'my masters, I have done nothing bad to this woman besides eating food. Is there any reason in this to make a woman leave her home?'

The elders: 'good gracious Bangunza! Man, is this how you have been treating your wife? O woman what a patient and forgiving person you must be to have lived with Bangunza and to have borne him children! You man there [the wife's brother], take your sister to your home. Bangunza, collect your spears [bridewealth]. What sort of ignominious man are you! Where is your dignity if you touch a woman's things before they are prepared and brought before you with proper respect? You pay five spears to her brother for the shameful things you have been doing to her.'

While Bangunza bowed his head in shame his wife fell before the elders and was sweeping dust from before them and throwing it at Bangunza.

MAN (DINGISO) AND WIFE (NABAATU) IN CULTIVATIONS

Nabaatu: 'oh Dingiso you clear this path to our cultivations; now we are wet to the skin when we pass along it in the dew. How shall we cultivate? This thick bush too which you have chosen. I don't know how we are going to get rid of it at all.'

Dingiso: 'child, which part of my strength will be spent in clearing the path and which in hoeing the cultivations? You can't skim dew from a person's body; we shall dry. Look you mistress, my father told me always to choose the thickest bush for cultivating and I would never lack food. Grass does not beat hard work.'

Nabaatu: 'ho ho! Your father could afford to do so because he had many wives. As for your situation, only you can find an answer to it. As I am often sick you will cultivate your bush by yourself, understand that! Mark out the piece we are to cultivate and don't waste time. As the sun will be hot soon, shall we hoe far? I shall soon return home to dry my soaked manioc in the sun. Does one cultivate crops with the energy of previous ones!'

Dingiso: 'Nabaatu, where did I throw the pole [for treading the grass down] yesterday? Look for it behind that termite mound over there. Brothers! Can wood disappear into the ground!'

Nabaatu: 'ho ho! And what about that pole right in front of you! Can't you see? Those Nile perches you used to eat along the river Yubu, their evil influence has followed after you [made you blind]. I am astonished at this, Bagi's daughter [herself], that a thing can be where anybody can see it and a person leaves here and searches for it everywhere else seems like foolishness to me.'

Dingiso: 'don't you know that I am quite advanced in age. . . .'

Nabaatu: 'old people do see you know! Bangatai here who excells at collecting caterpillars in these big forests here. . . . Be careful how you tread that thing my dear; you crush thorny branches as though you were walking in your courtyard; don't you know that a short tree-stump can pierce the foot of a cultivator? I speak because it is tiresome to look after a sick person.'

Dingiso: 'throw my hoe here and my matchet. On which side are you standing? I am taking my usual position! Have you ever seen a woman taking a position on the outer-edge of the marked-out piece of land?' [Later] 'we have done almost enough today, we will start on another piece again and when we finish it you can go home to roast some manioc [make a meal] while I cut down some of that terrible thorny bush we have met with. If we cultivate as much tomorrow our cultivations will get larger, and when we take it from there the day after tomorrow and push it forward anybody happening to pass by here will say, "people are indeed scratching the ground here." '

Nabaatu: 'you know, talking of how much you will cultivate took Ndege nowhere; perhaps your father did not tell you the story. He would go to his cultivations and mount a termite mound and survey his cultivations and say, "today we shall finish hoeing the grass up to yonder mound. By evening that mahogany tree will be standing in the cultivation. Tomorrow we shall bring that termite-mound into it. Now, Ndege's wives, cultivate this piece from here up to there. I shall come back and find you forward. I am going to court; the prince said yesterday that I should come early to consult his poison oracle." Did Ndege cultivate again after this his talk? When you are planning how you will cultivate make sure of the person who will assist you in the cultivating.'

Dingiso: 'Do you know Ndege's clan? He was a Gbambi. People of our clan do not fool about work. My father attracted people because of what his right hand secured for him. Elders like him used to await him in the evening at his fireside [for food].'

Nabaatu: 'if indeed it was your father who started a cultivation in such a fertile place he would build a second granary this year. A person takes after his father with his blessing, but what happened to you? You are like a person whose father did not bless him when he died!'

Dingiso: 'my father blest me more than my elder brothers because he died in my arms while they were in their homes. It is only that our evil neighbours have stolen the buds of our crops with their witchcraft. I have given them food in vain.'

Nabaatu: 'it is the mean person whose crops flourish. If you are not mean with food it is you whose crops people bewitch. Look at my maternal uncle Pazuo. Whenever a person tastes his food that person always rubs a bit of it on his knees.[1] People's crops fail but when you go to Pazuo's home you see his crops like wild grass. I am discussing it while this idle boy is coming.'

Dingiso: [to the boy] 'you lazy beast, you will die on account of people's property after my death.' [To the wife] 'what sort of rotten person is this thing to whom I have stressed the importance of work in vain? You will see young boys like him working with their fathers and it seems that I have no son after me who is mature and capable of work.' [To the boy] 'man, are you growing downwards? While I look this way take a matchet and go behind your mother and lop off branches from that tree I cut down yesterday.'

Nabaatu: 'when people talk about work he looks grim and puffs out his belly.' [To the boy] 'what has now filled your belly, was it grown by elephants? Where is Nangbara?'

Their son: 'she was boiling gourds and beans to bring them here.'

Dingiso: 'so you were waiting to fill your stomach with them before coming? That sister of yours is like you. A man does not take his character from a woman; I see this only in you. You will be a lazy man and she too will be a lazy woman. While women will be divorcing you because of your laziness men will be divorcing her away from their homes because of her laziness.'

Nabaatu: 'why do you tire your mouth? She will realize it after our death. My mother did not force me to go to the cultivations. On the contrary, they used to send me away from the cultivations to go home and boil gourds for them. If I had not accustomed

1. To prevent boils, since he has eaten a mean person's food.

myself to hard work I would now often go begging people to
give me this or that. As people do not cut two bunches of bananas
from their relatives[1] what would I do when they were tired of me?'

THE WIVES OF BAGU AND SENDEGO

Bagu's wife: 'oh my sister have you started your groundnuts
cultivation?'

Sendego's wife: 'we have done a little bit, being lazy people.
Sendego has been ill this year; it was only the day before yesterday
that he attempted to go to the cultivations as everybody has started
cultivating. What shall we do with the children we have? Bagu
has always been very active, so I dare say you have already started
the groundnuts cultivation.'

Bagu's wife: 'that is what he used to do before. Last year we
planted groundnuts very early and when Azande opened their eyes
and saw them our names were on their lips till thieves came and
stole all the groundnuts we had stored in the granary in abundance.
This year, knowing that it is time for work, they have given him
back-trouble [sickness]; he cuts into the ground once and sits
down. Let them grow plenty of groundnuts this year so that our
names may vanish from their mouths.'

Sendego's wife: 'as for Baimuke and his wives, they will plant
the first crop of groundnuts this month. He is such a hard worker!
He has started his cultivations very far at the head of the Nangume
stream. We came across it by chance the other day when we went
to look for salt plants to cut them down and burn them to get salt
out of them before heavy rains come. Sister, the cultivation of
the man and his wife was like that of a prince. You could suppose
that elephants had hoed it for him.'

Bagu's wife: 'he and his wife are fond of gossiping against people
about their cultivations. That short woman whom you see and
who speaks like a bee, she is a great gossip. Don't be deceived by
her pleasant talk and her joking. She is a nasty person.'

Sendego's wife: 'can you describe her to me? Was she not
gossiping against me, saying, we went fishing together and only I
caught plenty of fish? She accused me as if I had prevented her
from fishing. She came and sat relating it to me and Mbaraza's

1. A Zande proverb.

sister very exaggeratedly but we only watched her lips as she spoke. Do I take part in people's petty gossip? As they are now cultivating a big groundnuts patch does anybody wish that they die?'

Sendego's wife: 'as for Ngario's wife, she has left her husband working and just gone off to her brother's home. Some people have tolerant husbands; if it were I who "crossed a stream over the bridge of the unfortunate man" where would I sit when I returned?'

Bagu's wife: 'didn't she do the same thing last year and Ngario planted all the groundnuts while she was away?'

Sendego's wife: 'my sister, what makes a man decide to marry another wife and then his wife refuses—she will go on causing him trouble. Isn't it that how it starts?'

Bagu's wife: 'as Bagu has been marrying his wives have I ever opened my mouth about it? I have always favoured it. Feeding a man is not an easy task. If another person comes to assist you, is that a bad thing? It is only the one who comes and wants to take your place that you have to remind that things are not like that.'

Sendego's wife: 'since *sere pasio* [groundnuts, sesame and other oil-bearing plants used as flavourings] did not grow well in my cultivations last year am I not suffering from lack of them this year like a dog? Oh my sister I thought of going to you for a little *kpagu* [an oil-bearing gourd] and sesame seed.'

Bagu's wife: 'you would have tired your legs to no purpose. The little I stored in a gourd for seed I gave to that lazy and stupid wife of my brother who looks for oil-seeds every wet season. If rats don't eat up the little that remains I shall give you a little of it. Seeds need not be many [to give a good crop]. Somebody will give you some more and it will push your cultivation a little further.'

Sendego's wife: 'oh my sister, that is very fortunate. Some *bangumbe* [an oil-bearing gourd] seed escaped the rats. Since you lack it send a child for a little of it. It is not good to lack such little things for oil-flavourings. A person soon becomes tired of eating groundnut flavouring.'

Bagu's wife: 'especially Bagu who like Sendego has the habit of saying he has lost all appetite for groundnuts!'

Sendego's wife: 'my sister, I have always been bored with that nonsense. Other men kill animals while it looks as though they have no nets to carry and no spears.'

Bagu's wife: 'I will not discuss that any more. The wet season has come again and I have not sliced meat and smeared myself with blood. We shall now have to eat manioc leaves with those who enjoyed meat in the dry season. I guess grass has grown to cover the animals and rain has caused the streams to rise and hide the fish.'

Sendego's wife: 'don't mention it! We shall be alike. Oh my sister, I am going home to see what might have happened there.'

Bagu's wife: 'let us sit and chat a little longer. Are there no people at home?'

Sendego's wife: 'my dear sister, I spread my manioc to dry and now the sun has set I am going to sweep it up. Since the children have all gone away from me to their relatives I now tire out like those who chase each other about. Sendego went to court this morning and may now be on his way back. Where will he find even mere water to drink?'

Bagu's wife: 'I will send Kutiyote with your little sesame seed tomorrow.'

Sendego's wife: 'oh yes, you will look in her hand for that thing I mentioned.'

ZAMAI, HIS WIFE NAKAYA AND THEIR LITTLE SON TORO

Toro: 'wa wa! O mother what shall we do with all these termites we have gathered? Have other people also gathered so many?'

Nakaya: 'that mouth of yours! When a person probes, you tell him that your father gathered plenty of termites! You boy with that pig-like mouth of yours, you are very indiscreet. A person will first cause a big boil in your throat before you realize the Azande you just see looking innocent are terrible people.'

Zamai: 'why do you tire your mouth? As you are his mother, you advise him. I can't figure out which god straightened [instructed] the children of past ages. What could you expect to hear from a child if you asked him in the season of termites: "oh no sir! My mother was ill yesterday so she was not active when the termites were swarming so hers escaped while she was on the way. My father's did not swarm at all though they bored many holes through the clay crust of their mounds. Those that took flight were just enough to go into a little bundle for [grinding and boiling into] a mash." '

Nakaya: 'after what the child has said you will not hear any-thing more from him.'

Toro: 'oh no, when a person asks me I will just tell him that all the termite mounds were deserted, so a person may not bewitch me, saying that we are enjoying termites.'

Zamai: 'so you know that people are bewitched for termites. These Azande will boast of the lots of termites they have caught, and next year will they boast of them? Nakaya weren't you here while Songodi was boasting of how he filled big baskets of termites last year? I thought it was that same time when his wife burst in upon us looking everywhere for termite wings, pretending that she had not gathered any termites.'

Nakaya: 'I am indeed going to her myself this year to ask her to give me some.'

Toro: 'mother I met her at the pool and she was covered with termite wings.'

Zamai: 'what did you say when she probed you thus?'

Toro: 'I said that we did not gather any termites. But she said with malice "do you ever go without termites?" '

Nakaya: 'may they rub fire in her mouth! She has gathered enough and thinks everybody has done so. . . . Toro take water to your father my little son and come and give him termites so that he may taste them. Binza died with a digdig's head in his bag.[1] When they say it is your father's "fire"[2] you make a fire belt round it.'

Zamai: 'ha! Termites are so plentiful in their season that one has no appetite for them. It is only after they are stored and are scarce that they become sweet. My dear, didn't you roast some manioc to be eaten with these termites?'

Nakaya: 'ha! Sorry, I had forgotten. Toro come and give your father manioc for his termites.'

A TALE: A HUSBAND AND YAM PEEL

A man's wife went to visit her mother and he followed some time later. He arrived at his in-laws at sunset and he was warmly wel-

1. Binza did not want his digdig's head cooked quickly so he went around with it in his bag and died without having eaten it.
2. Fire (we) has here the sense of bush preserved against the annual firing for later hunting.

comed by them and by his wife. He sat by the fire with his father-in-law and two other young men who were paying a visit. While they were seated boiled yam was brought, but the son-in-law did not eat it with the others.

When the two young men had gone the women came to the fireplace to chat. They left their salt on the fire boiling *kpo, kpo, kpo*.[1] The son-in-law thought it was their porridge being cooked, so he was happy and talking contentedly. But when it was getting late his mother-in-law yawned sleepily and addressed her daughter, 'child, take that salt off the fire.' When he heard that he nearly fell off his stool and he began to regret having refused the yam.

When people had gone to bed he could not sleep. He was ill-tempered and quarrelsome with his wife. After a little while he darted out of the hut and ran to the fireplace. It was about to rain and there was much lightning. With each flash he swooped upon a piece of yam peel and began to eat some bits of yam left on it.

When he had not returned his wife was puzzled and she put out her head to look for him. She saw him in the flashes of lightning gathering up yam peel at the fireplace. When he returned she cried angrily, 'why is mother taking so long preparing this thing?' With that, she rushed out. The man was greatly perplexed and wondered what his mother-in-law was doing. 'Is it possible' he thought, 'that my mother-in-law is cooking food for me and I have been degrading myself by eating yam peel?'

His wife went at once to her mother and wakened her and told her the story. So they took boiled meat and prepared a meal in a great hurry. While the mother was cooking porridge her daughter was preparing a meaty flavouring to go with it. After a short time she hurried with the meal to her husband in the hut, saying, 'my brother, my mother is now old, she used to be able to cook fast.'

So he got up and helped himself. But in the morning he was puzzled. He felt certain he had been seen gathering yam peel, so whenever the women giggled in the kitchen that day he believed they were making fun of him.

So we say, 'what had been put before you do not leave it hoping for something better ahead.'

1. They were extracting salt by boiling salty marsh plants.

A TALE: A MOTHER AND DAUGHTER

A woman went to visit her married daughter to eat things there. She carried many kinds of food to her daughter in a big basket. The day she arrived her daughter and her daughter's husband were very happy.

When she had spent ten days there her son-in-law went hunting. He returned at dusk while his wife was at the stream. When she returned she went into her hut to see what her husband had brought from the bush. On looking into her big beer-pot she saw something like a python. She kept quiet and went outside rejoicing in her heart.

When it was dark there was bright moonshine like sunlight. So the daughter got up, saying, 'what bright moonlight! A mother could go right to her home in it.' When her mother heard this she did not like it. So she got up to go home. She thought, 'why is my daughter chasing me away from her home?' In vain did her son-in-law try to turn her back, in vain did he beg her to spend the night with them and depart in the morning. She refused and insisted on departing at once, so at last he decided to accompany her as her home was far.

No sooner had they departed than her daughter rushed headlong into her hut and made for her big beer-pot and plunged in her hand to bring out her python. Instead, a cobra raised its head and bit her hand and she screamed. Her husband and her mother heard her cry out and when they returned in haste they found her at the point of death. She then related the cause of her death, and her husband dashed into the hut and killed the cobra. Her mother said to her 'o my daughter, were you chasing me away on account of a snake?' While she was still speaking her daughter died.

That is why we say, 'don't chase your relative away on account of food. Meanness is bad.'

ABOUT A WITCH-DOCTOR'S DANCE

Gburadi: 'in whose home are they dancing this witch-doctors' dance?' His wife: 'do I know anything about sponsors of witch-doctors' dances? May be they are dancing to heal Susu's sister. Aren't you going there to consult about us?'

His brother: 'do I like attending witch-doctors' dances? I attended one the other day and the witch-doctor Siata started the nonsense that my father has spoilt my chances of marriage. What should I have done to my father that should make him spoil my life?'

The wife: 'are you a witch? It is only a witch who is apprehensive at a witch-doctor's dance!'

The brother: 'have I ever bewitched you?'

The wife: 'I have often been sick here anyway. These bachelors you see around always cast a bad eye on other people's wives.'

The brother: 'if you talk like that I shall soon bewitch you.'

The wife: 'you will see who will cook for you. When witch-doctors want to straighten out the problem of women for you you say they are talking nonsense, you will continue carrying your own water yourself. Don't you know that that old father of yours has witchcraft in that big belly of his, do you imagine that it is beauty that makes him fat?'

Gburadi: 'you are talking like this in his absence. He too knows how to insult people. He is a master of wit.'

The wife: 'what is there "in his mouth" besides the talk of old age!'

The brother: 'all right, I shall go today to the witch-doctors to have my marriage problem sorted out by them. If I don't marry a girl this year nobody will again see me attending a witch-doctor's dance.'

Gburadi: 'if it is Wiriwiri, he dances well [is a clever witch-doctor]. Is it not he who dug up a fowl's wing under a bed in Yangu's home?'

The wife: 'oh yes, the fowl's wing Yangu's wife hid from him that he might not confront her brother with it.[1] oh that woman is a strange character. Why should a woman interfere with men's fowls' wings?'

The brother: 'and why should men consult the poison oracle about their brothers-in-law?' It seems anyhow that she and her brother had joined together to bewitch Yangu.'

A child: 'I say father, how did he know the fowl's wing was under the bed?'

1. The wing of a fowl which had died to her brother's name in a consultation of the poison oracle.

The brother: 'by his ash [magical medicine] of course. Do you think witch-doctors play? Yangu summoned the witch-doctors to discover the source of his death [sickness]. He knew that his wife and her brother were the cause of his trouble. You see child, the man [witch-doctor] danced here and there where his magic had stirred in him, and before long he called Yangu in a loud voice and told him to open the door of his wife's hut. At this, Yangu's wife was trembling.'

The wife: 'very characteristic of a witch, his heart is always in his hand [he is always worried].'

The brother: 'when the witch-doctor rushed out of the hut we saw the fowl's wing in his hand. He danced and hovered [sprang about] with it in his hand while people bowed their heads and suddenly he planted it before Yangu's brother-in-law. He raised his hand and let it down and the drummers stopped beating on gong and drums. Gasping for breath, he strode to where Yangu's wife was sitting. All eyes were turned on her.'

A child: 'what a wonderful clever witch-doctor!'

The brother: 'looking her in the face, he demanded of her the reason why she had Yangu's fowl's wing under the bed.'

The wife: 'if it had been me I would have dried up [died] with shame.'

The brother: 'there is no shame in a confirmed witch's eyes. The woman told him on the spot that she had hidden it to prevent Yangu from giving it to humiliate her brother with it. Looking directly into her eyes, Siata asked her and her brother why they were "killing" Yangu. The woman and her brother were gazing up at the sky.'

Gburadi: 'he was bewitched because of that digdig he killed and carried it entire to his new wife.'

The brother: 'that is what Siata and the others revealed to them.'

A child: 'what did they say?'

The brother: 'what else could they say except that their hearts were burning for that meat?'

A child: 'please finish [what you are doing] so that we may go there.'

The wife: 'as you are so restless don't tire my mouth today. At a witch-doctors' dance a child should go and sit at the feet of his father or mother and should not run about here and there.'

The brother: 'if you stand up often the witch-doctors will cast a spell on you. So children, though other people's children dart about in the crowd, you stay by us.'

A child: 'hi, Toro and the others think they are youths, let them go and run about [among the people], the witch-doctors will cast a spell on them.'

Toro: 'well, but you are the one who plays rough games at funerals. Be careful today.'

Another child: 'I won't go away from my father's side.'

Gburadi: 'if anyone gets up, there is the witch-doctors' spell they cast on noisy children.'

ABOUT COTTON CLOTHES

Bawiri and his wife Ruta converse at home in the evening after their return from the market.

Ruta: 'Ngatuo's wives dressed themselves today in new cotton dresses. My word, those who earn money are lucky. Especially Natumbagi; when things are like that she struts about like a prince's mother-in-law.'

Bawiri: 'was their big cotton harvest just a joke?'

Ruta: 'do you mean they have bought all these clothes with only the cotton money? A "world" of groundnuts and eleusine flourished for them this year and many people have been flocking there to buy these things. The way to their home is worn down by bicycles and shoes this year. What can you think of people whose crops abound as if they grew in a dead man's estate? If it were I, one bicycle would come and I would sweep the granary clean.'

Bawiri: 'if you fix your mind on these cotton prints which have filled the shops will you eat anything again? You will sell everything so that you may dress like others.'

Ruta: 'but no! A big man like you who also cultivates like others should also have a good suit of clothes to appear in among his neighbours during gatherings. People have left off wearing blankets and of course I can't mention the bark cloth which has been abandoned to widows and widowers! Buy a good pair of shorts and a shirt for yourself sometime soon, it is shameful to go without good clothes.'

Bawiri: 'child, if I had kept all the money I have spent on hashish and meat would I be talking of clothes again?'

Ruta: 'when I talk to you about clothes you make fun of it, but don't you realize that a person also wears clothes while eating meat and smoking hashish? While you are making yourself foolish I am going soon to brew beer to buy a skirt and a black sheet of cloth with the money I shall earn from the sale of the beer.'

Bawiri: 'haven't you been told that your friends have discarded the black sheet of cloth and skirt? They wear frocks these days as you see them in them in the market place. Work for money in order to buy a good cotton print.'

Ruta: 'hii, am I a young girl again to wear frocks my dear? Where will I find money for it? As for my black sheet, I can wrap it about me by day and at night cover my nose with it from mosquitoes.'

Bawiri: 'that is true my sister, I will take it from you to wear when you are not going to the market.'

Ruta: 'oh no! No! That shameful thing men have taken to wearing their wives' black sheet of cloth is a thing I will not tolerate in you. To wear it as Sambia stood unbecomingly in Nagirimbiro's cloth today! I wonder how their wives are not ashamed of them; if it were I where might I look on account of that shameful thing? No sir, buy men's clothes that are so abundant in the shops.'

Bawiri: 'well, if a person is in a fix why should he not put on his wife's garments? Sambia wore his wife's today; did he die? Just admit it is you who do not at all want me to wear your black cloth. Anyway, I have my bark cloth which my fathers used to wear.'

Ruta: 'when he is told the right thing he says childish things in reply. Are women's clothes for men? Is this the age of your fathers and bark cloth? Did your fathers grow cotton?'

Bawiri: 'you buy for me then like the others!'

Ruta: 'by our graves [a woman's oath], if I have money I can buy it; and it is for a careless lazy attitude towards yourself, people can visit you in numbers just to see what sort of man you are.'

Bawiri: 'Baru's children have brought clothes from Nzara in which they are showing off like butterflies.'

Ruta: 'that is why they run to the towns. As laziness has got the upper hand of them they can't set foot in the cultivations after their parents but its tomorrow to Nzara and the next day to Yambio. What will happen when that type marries, as growing cotton is a tough business!'

Bawiri: 'you talk about an old idea. Remove your hunting net from behind [forget the old idea—you are living in the past]. They are going to be married to men at Nzara where people work for money. Those, you see, simply desire to wash their feet thoroughly in the morning, take their little Juba baskets that have been introduced to them, and enter the market place and say "how much is that? Oh no lady, the price of your flour is too high." Is there anything else they want?'

Ruta: 'that is a shameful thing. Is the main reason why girls flock to the towns fear of cultivating in the villages?'

Bawiri: 'the "bone" [core] is the desire for cotton prints and shoes. When they see others coming from town in beautiful clothes and shoes they say there is the centre of good things. The desire to dress well is so much in the heart of people, especially women, that it is no longer a plaything. Weren't you present the other day during sleeping-sickness inspection when Nzari's wife brought a case against him before the headmen?'

Ruta: 'did she complain that Anzari had never bought clothes for her?'

Bawiri: 'she asserted that all her married life with Nzari she had never put her hand under his for even a handkerchief. She wears leaves while other women wear good clothes.'

Ruta: 'did the headmen buy it for her?'

Bawiri: 'they bought it for her when cotton was sold. When people sold the early cotton the princes summoned Nzari on the spot my dear and told him just to place his cotton money before the court first. They divided it there and his wife took her share and made for the shops while Nzari took his and went after his drinks and hashish with it.'

Ruta: 'I'll leave my case aside and discuss his! Since the white men came whoever has seen Nzari really well dressed and people inquiring who he was when he approached them?'

Bawiri: 'his best garment, which is a sheet which he passes between his legs, what can push it away from him anywhere? Look you, there are some of us who are in great poverty in the midst of all these European goods.'

Ruta: 'if a person is determined to cultivate do you think he will be poor? What is there that does not bring you in money these days? Even sweet potatoes, they are money too.'

Bawiri: 'how can you work with all these witches around? If

you do simple cultivation today they will say you are trying to raise your head among them. Owing to this jealousy they will knock you down with some severe malady and only God will save you from them. And when you want to try again to cultivate the season of cultivating will have passed.'

Ruta: 'anyway, people do their work all the same in spite of these witches. Did they tell you a person is God?'

WIDOWS

There is no poorer person among the Azande than a widow [or widower]. When a person's spouse dies, from the day of death till after the burial the widow cannot even drink water. It is only after the burial that the relatives of the dead put water to the lips of the spouse. It is well that women wail near the body for only one night and in the morning the body is buried. Then the widow may drink water.

When she [or he] has taken water the entire property of the household is assembled, even food such as eleusine and groundnuts, and seeds of all kinds. These things are then divided among the relatives of the dead and of the widow [the relatives take the major share]. Not even a small pot is left. The senior relatives take the more important things and the junior ones carry away small things.

After they have built a hut over the grave the relatives of the dead man will take his widow to a stream after her head has been shaved. At the stream she is stripped of her entire attire, including her waist-string, and washed thoroughly. Then they tie a new string round her waist and dress her in new undyed bark cloth [and only new bark cloth for a widower]. After taking her out of the stream, she does not go back to the old home again. Until death she will never put foot in that place again [it is the same for a widower], for if she goes to the old home she will become obese and stupid.

The grave is left till a senior relative of the dead plants a large cultivation and collects lots of meat. He then gives a big feast at which the in-laws erect a pile of stones on the grave, and people eat, drink beer, and dance for two days.

A widower makes a new homestead for himself and his children if he has only one wife. If he has several wives they all enter their new home together. He then begins to gather household property afresh. The co-wives of the dead woman keep their old property but the husband does not eat from these old food utensils [so they prefer to exchange them where possible], nor of any food they bring from the old homestead.

In the past a widow would go and live near her dead husband's mother's son. This man would get together utensils for her and he would cultivate for her [and her children] while she was mourning. He would also look after his brother's children well.

In the past a woman used to mourn for her husband for two or three years. After that time the mourning would be lifted from her. In most cases she then married this brother-in-law who had looked after her. If she had no brother-in-law she would go to live in the home of a good sister's son of her dead husband or of some other kind relative of her husband. Widows rarely went to live with their own relatives.

During the period of mourning the widow or widower does not eat things just anyhow. She does not eat in people's homes from their old pots because she may not eat flavouring of ladies' fingers or the flesh of elephant and bushbuck. She may not eat from the pots in which these things are cooked. When the widow is living in such poverty and misery the relatives of the dead appoint a woman among them who is to anoint the widow with oil at the end of the period of mourning. In the old days this woman secured oil of the *akiedo* termites and she ground *kurukpu* dye. After that she looked for a new couch and mat, after which she would dye black a good piece of bark cloth, and she looked for a good *agbaya* apron for dressing up the widow. She would also fetch ornaments for the widow. For a widower she would find a large stretch of dyed bark cloth and a good straw hat.

After that beer is brewed, plenty of food cooked, and people gather to see the widow being relieved of mourning [for the first time since the death of her husband] and to eat and drink. In the afternoon she is taken to a stream after her hair, if a woman, has been plaited [for the first time since the death of her husband]. In the past some men used to have their hair plaited like women. When they return with the widow from the stream she is dressed in her new attire and seated on a new stool with a new mat for her feet. After that she is anointed with oil [together with *kurukpu* dye if a widow]. While this is going on men and women put money beside her. In the past these gifts consisted of ornaments, knives, good spears, and hoes too. These things are left for the widow when people disperse. After that the widow lives like other people. This termination of the mourning period is done when the magic to kill those responsible for the dead man's death has done its work.

When a relative is mourning for the dead he, or she, does not abstain from many things like a widow does, but he does not wear bark cloth nor does he anoint himself with oil, and he shaves his head regularly. When he wants to end his mourning he prepares eleusine for beer, collects plenty of meat, and summons people to come and dance in his homestead. This takes place after the magic for avenging the death has done its work. If at the same time the person wants to erect a memorial pile of stones on the grave he gives a feast (as I have described before). Things are gathered to take away his pollution (*giro*) just as in the case of a widow. He is washed in the afternoon of the day the dance finishes, and when he is being anointed with oil people throw money down beside him. After that he gets up to dance and when people join in to show their happiness at the event the dance swells till the sun sets.

FATHER AND SON (ABOUT CULTIVATING)

Father: 'e my son, as the time of cultivation has come and your comrades are cutting down the forest, when will you start cutting yours?'

Son: 'sir I will cut it after sharpening my matchet and axe.'

Father: 'you should cut it down during this last warm weather so that it can be burnt before the heavy rains, because last year you planted groundnuts late and they did not do well.'

Son: 'very good, sir, I will go tomorrow in the morning to the blacksmith to sharpen my tools.'

Father: 'but where are you going to cultivate this year since where you cultivated last year was not a good place?'

Son: 'I don't know a good place where I can cultivate this year father. But I am thinking of cultivating just at the edge of the fallow ground I cultivated last year and abandoned it at the path which is between us there and the man Ngbaya.'

Father: 'don't cultivate there this year, because crops were not fruitful in it last year.'

Son: 'where then should I cultivate sir?'

Father: 'I think you should cultivate in the forest of *banga* trees which is between you and the man Mangunomaru.'

Son: 'yes, sir, I was thinking of cultivating there this year, but when I consulted my wife about it she told me that pigs play havoc with the crops in that place.'

Father: 'what pigs man? Just cultivate in the place I have shown you. If pigs begin eating things put up a small hut there for sleeping in so as to drive them away by night.'

Son: 'o father, since I sleep heavily who will drive them away for me? A woman cannot come out at night alone.'

Father: 'man stop that stupid talk about who will scare the animals from the crops for you at night. Look you, when I was a young man no animal could eat my crops; from where would that animal come? Because if animals ate something of mine that would mean missing sleep to drive them away.'

Son: 'that is true father, I am going to do as you say. It is better to try something than to look at it with the eyes, only.'

Father: 'but before you cultivate in that place you should first find out your condition [consult the oracles]; as you are going to cultivate there and go there with the people of your home to protect things from animals, nothing bad will happen to you? For if it [the oracle] says your family will not be fortunate there, then cultivate the edge of the fallow you thought of before.'

Son: 'o father, about consulting oracles. I have given that up because the preacher told us that we should not consult oracles any more since we are believers in [subjects of] God.'

Father: 'boy, some of these things are all nonsense. It was God who gave us all these things and told us to do them. Why do you say that a preacher said it is not right for us to consult the oracles?'

Son: 'look sir, my father, God does not want bad things, because things like consulting the poison oracle are all of Satan.'

Father: 'right you are my son! Is it so? Look, age is coming on me terribly. You should put me right my son, because in the past we used to honour gods at sources of streams.'

Son: 'yes indeed father, you should be going to church on Sunday to worship God and to listen to the good news which is written in the Book of God, because it is God who gives rain to make our things grow.'

Father: 'yes my son, when Sunday comes remind me so that we may go to hear God's words and what the Bible says about consulting oracles.'

Son: 'very good father, now I am going home to take my tools tomorrow morning to the blacksmiths for sharpening.'

Father: 'boy, you sharpen those tools tomorrow as quickly as you can to cut down the bush in this cultivation before the heavy rains set in.'

Son: 'yes sir. Where will you cultivate this year yourself?'

Father: 'I cannot hoe any more boy. All my bones are diseased. Only your mothers are cultivating the edge of the fallow where they planted groundnuts last year.'

Son: 'good-bye father.'

Father: 'good-bye to you my son.'

Son: 'when my mother returns from the cultivations tell her that I greet her warmly. When eating some things on Thursday they should keep some for me.'

TALKS IN THE HOME ON FAMILY AFFAIRS

A man is in his home with his wife, or maybe two wives, together with his children—daughters and sons. The duty of the daughters is to be in the kitchen with their mother to help her in cooking while that of the sons is to be with their father in the evenings by the fire to listen to what strong words he has to say about things. On a day when the father and his sons sit alone without guests being present their conversation goes like this:

Father: 'boys, as I have begotten four of you and three daughters, hold your own among strangers and do not be against one another.'

A son: 'father, since we are four here on the one hand and on the other hand there are only three girls how shall we manage to share their bridewealth between all of us?'

Father: 'do not bicker about girls' affairs. Since there are only three girls and four of you, you, Sasa, you are the last born and you will have to go without bridewealth. Leave it to your older brothers. The three of you, Mange, Rikita and Mboto, you are to

share the bridewealth of the three girls. But each of you in turn
have to contribute some money to help Sasa, your last born
brother, because he has no sister's bridewealth to marry with.'

Sasa: 'o father, as you have said thus, what shall I do if after
you have died Mange, Rikita and Mboto are nasty with me and
refuse to give me money for marriage?'

Father: 'Mange, since you are the first born, if you do not get a
wife for this Sasa, your youngest brother, after I have died my
spirit will fall on you and nobody will be able to appeal to me on
your behalf. I warn you to be careful, for when I die I shall still
keep a watch on you all. And now there is another matter, for I
see you doing something which is very bad, and that is that when
people come to our home here and they are given food to eat you
hover around near them looking at them like dogs, and when they
feel embarrassed they invite you to eat together with them.
Furthermore, when you are invited to eat, instead of eating
decently with them and having respect for their hands you mess
up their hands in the broth. I do not like this behaviour and it is
odious to my spirit. It is a habit of barbarians and it is a very bad
one. When decent people come to our home and they are given
food, you boys must not stand hanging about them. Go and play
your games out of sight. If they are people with any sense, when
they have more than enough food they will give you what is left
over for you to eat. Even if they eat all of it, never mind, there is
your mother who will think of you and cook you some food later
for you to eat. And do not treat the matter lightly, it is the cause
of death of many boys, because if there is a witch among those
people and he has not satisfied himself with the food before he
gives it to you he will be annoyed and will bewitch a boy to death
or cause to be revealed to him wild cats [*adandara*] so that he dies
at once. Another thing is this: it is not good to go after the wives
of other people. When you grow up to manhood look for a woman
to marry her.'

Mboto: 'I forgot, father, I was going to tell you that I want to
marry that girl, the daughter of Babiro.'

Father: 'o my son, that is not the sort of girl even an orphan
would marry. She is not a decent girl. All the time she plays with
young men. She does not help her mother in the kitchen and she
will be a lazy person in the future. When last I went to her father's
home and ate food which she had cooked it was tasteless, there

was almost no salt in the broth; the porridge was more or less uncooked as if the flour had been poured into cold water. She married a man before and the man said that she ate all the meat and left only the bones. She is not an upright girl. She likes to put on a lot of dresses and shoes to show off before official people. If you marry her where will you get money to buy clothes like that? In the morning she washes only her feet and puts on shoes and goes to the market. If she went this morning to the market she would just be looking at and admiring the men in the market without going home until everybody else had left the market; then she would go home. Is that the habit of a proper woman? What about her husband—what will he do for hunger at home? If you marry that girl my son she will not in the future entertain your relatives. She is the kind of woman who looks down on the kin of the home, as smooth as a lake. I don't think she would bring out food even for guests. She always cooks in very small quantities if she does bring out food at all. How can the people eat it? O my children, you ought to marry women who are decent!'

Mboto: 'how does a person know a decent woman, father?'

Father: 'a decent woman is a woman who regards people with respect. She is active in the home. When many people come to the home she goes around smiling and without a frown on her face. A decent woman is one who, when people come to the home, would at once cook regardless whether she has just cooked before, and she will not complain that she is tired. A decent woman is one who, when a relative of her husband dies goes there at once to wail.

'And also for you the husband, do not cook in her absence with the remainder of her flour. A good man is one who does not search his wife's place. He does not count what he gives to the wife [to cook]. He does not consume the remainder of the wife's food— that is a shameful thing to do. A man who insults a wife is not a good husband. Better the man who beats a wife instead of insulting her. A good husband is one who respects his mother-in-law, who cuts firewood for his mother-in-law, and who visits his in-laws at funerals. O my sons, if you do not do likewise you will not marry.'

MOTHER AND DAUGHTERS

A mother, the mistress of the home, sits with her three daughters in the kitchen cooking and she admonishes them thus:

Mother: 'Look here girls, I have noticed that you have now the habit of taking food and sitting with it in the middle of the homestead and eating it openly. Even when men come you do not enter a hut with the food but continue eating so that they see your mouths, eating food. We did not do that sort of thing when we were girls. A girl should conceal herself from boys while eating. A girl is not supposed to eat openly in front of a man.'

Nareke: 'Mother, when a man marries me should I continue to conceal myself from him when eating?'

Mother: 'Not at all. When a man has just married you, you should not eat openly in front of him. Even when you go to live with him you have to wait for about two to three years until you get to know him intimately. By that time, if your husband loves you very much, one day when he is having a meal he will call you and put some money down before you and he will tell you to eat openly in front of him on that money. Then you will take the money and take a bite openly in front of him. Usually this takes place at bedtime. After this you will continue to eat openly in his presence but you will still not eat in the presence of other men. A woman continues to abstain from food in the sight of men until she has borne several children, perhaps three or four. But in these modern times, since the plane flew over our girls, they do not observe all these things. All the girls act as if they were immature.

'In the past girls did not eat such animals as iguana, wild cat, all monkeys, and ant-bear. Do not eat these animals I have just mentioned—women do not eat them for they are for you unclean animals. Even if your husband persuades you to eat them, do not do so; for he is just testing you to see your character. If you eat unclean beasts he will divorce you or make a fool of you by composing a song against you.

'Another thing again: when you get married do not cook a bird and divide it. That is one of the worst things. Birds of all kinds, when cooked, must not be divided. If your husband brings you a chicken, a guinea-fowl, a francolin or any other kind of bird cook it and give it to him whole with the pot for him to eat it, without any part of it missing. Do not take part of it for yourself but cook for yourself ordinary vegetables to eat with the porridge. If he is a good man he himself will put some of the meat into a leaf and call you to take it and eat it, but if he does not give you some of it do not mind about it.

'Still another matter is that when a woman is menstruating she must not eat an animal which has been killed by a gun and she must not touch her husband's spears or sit on his seat or bed. She must sleep on a separate bed. The woman who goes to bed with a man when she is menstruating is a stupid woman and the man will at once divorce her. If you eat the meat of an animal killed by a gun when you are menstruating it will kill you because guns have spells on them.'

AN OLD MAN TALKS TO HIS SONS ABOUT PAST AND PRESENT

Boys, you have been born into a better world than ours. You, my sons, and all of you have taken to dress in European cloth. Men have stopped dressing in bark cloth and now dress in sewn shorts and shirts and even shoes. The women have stopped wearing leaves and have taken to skirts, frocks, and some of them even wear shoes. There were none of these things in the old days. Our cloth which we wore was bark cloth, and the women just used leaves. Young men like you were sewing bark cloth into shorts just like your shorts nowadays, and they made shirts too.[1] They dyed the bark cloth nicely black to make it very soft. Especially when there was a dance, young men and elderly men would dress so well that it would be hard to distinguish the one who should be sent to get fire for the other.[2] We would plait our hair and dye it red so that when we walked to the dance the women would file behind us. Of those who watch only the women would raise their heads, the men would bend theirs.[3] O my children, what I am telling you is true, otherwise somebody would have sneezed by now. But today you have to get money, up to sixty piastres to buy

1. This may have been so after I had left Zandeland but it was not so when I was there. Then there was nothing which could have been described as shorts and shirts.
2. An inferior is sent to get fire for lighting a smoke.
3. This means that men will be envious of the turn-out of their fellows whereas the women will admire them.

a good pair of shorts, and even then women will not pay attention to you unless you earn still more to buy a shirt to go over the shorts. Only then will you look like a well-to-do person. If you fail to do this you will not be a person at all. You will be going about in a loin-cloth. My children, that is where it is really difficult for you. It is not so bad now that a work town, Nzara, has been established for spinning and weaving.[1] Nowadays it is common for young men to go to Nzara for work and when you come across a young man today and ask him:

'Where are you going?'
'I am going to look for work in Nzara.'
'What about you?'
'I too am going to Nzara.'
'And that one over there?'
'He also is going to Nzara.'

All the young men want to go to Nzara to look for paid work for it is difficult to find money for clothes, and if a man stays idle what will he do? In order to dress well a person must earn not less than a pound and fifty piastres.

Villagers[2] in general who are elderly and cannot travel about as young men do get their money in cultivating cotton. For a person who is a bachelor, the field-officers[3] allot him one feddan, and a married man will be alloted two feddans. If you have from two to three wives you get three feddans. A man whose cotton cultivation is in really good fertile soil may get a really good yield of cotton and make thirty pounds a year; but an average earning for many people is fifteen pounds. Out of this money you have to pay tax which is a pound nowadays. In the past the tax was only five piastres a head. After paying the tax you have to give money to your wives for them to buy dresses. If there is anything left over after all that you take it for yourself to buy your clothes, a pair of

1. An industrial township established some fifteen miles from the old government centre at Yambio. It was founded to be the industrial side to an attempt by the government of the Anglo-Egyptian Sudan at agricultural development (in my opinion an ill-considered and disastrous one). See Conrad C. Reining, *The Zande Scheme*, 1966, *passim.*
2. 'Villagers'—the Zande is *aboro lingara*, which in the old days would have meant those who did not frequent court. See *ibid.* for what it came to mean.
3. See *ibid.* A host of agricultural overseers appear to have descended on the Azande like a plague.

shorts and a shirt. Then you pay further bridewealth for your wives with the rest of the money and await next year's yield.

HOW THE YOUNG MEN LIVED

The mature young men built separate huts for themselves near their fathers' homesteads. The younger ones built huts in which two, three, or four might sleep. Sometimes ashes accumulated in the younger boys' hut due to such foolishness as 'I gathered up the ashes yesterday, you do it today.' 'No, I swept the hut the day before, so-and-so is sweeping it today.' The mature young men forced the boys to sweep their huts. Boys slept on beds covered with leaves. The young men slept on beds or couches covered with mats. They too could beat bark cloth for covering themselves.

Early in the morning all the young men used to go to the cultivations of the elder to hoe them. So they would labour until the heat was intense. So one of the elder's wives would go home to boil gourd, maize, beans or earthnuts which she would bring to the cultivations. Sometimes she would cook a lot of porridge into big wooden bowls with flavouring in a big pot which she would carry to the cultivations [with the help of one of her daughters]. The people would stop work to eat, then after a short rest they would fall to work again till the late afternoon.

Since by day people ate in the cultivations it was difficult for a lazy person to eat by day. So the young men would all go to the cultivations, even the lazy ones. When the sun went down the women tied bundles of firewood to carry home for cooking. The elder would also go home with his young men to wash off 'the earth of cultivation'. In the evening the young men would go to sit by the elder's fire to await food. While they were waiting for food the elder would admonish them or tell them stories of the old days. Sometimes he would leave them to tell their folk-tales. After the meal they would wait for the elder to go to bed before they went to their huts.

Sometimes the wives would not send enough food to the fire-place, so many young men would go to sleep on an empty stomach. Boys would eat with their mothers. The young men too could go to eat in their mother's kitchen. But the young man who had no mother there, if another of his father's wives did not kindly give him a little food, he would spend the night hungry. The young men had no cultivations of their own because they had no hoes [or axes]. A young man got married and then the elder [his father] gave him implements. The young men performed many duties for the elder—cultivating, carrying his hunting nets to hunt for him—and the elder would often send them on errands. The men who were married to a single wife used to cultivate in the same manner as those with several wives. If there were no young men around his homestead he would cultivate with his wife alone.

We say thus, 'if you are on a journey and darkness finds you on your way, do not spend the night in a big homestead. Go to a small homestead where there is only one wife; then you will not sleep on an empty stomach.' We say so because in a big homestead one wife says, 'I supplied food to his fireplace yesterday. She in whose hut he slept last night, let her cook for him.' While they talk thus the elder sleeps with hunger.

WEALTH

A wealthy man was one whose granaries were full and in whose homestead there was no hunger. There was plenty of manioc in the grass around his homestead and many banana trees thick around. The elder who had many daughters, many sisters, and many female relatives dependent on him would become rich from their bridewealth. If the prince was generous to him and made him gifts, these would enrich him. So youths and bachelors were poor. Those elders who had only one wife could not grow as wealthy as those with many wives; but they could fill their granaries if they were very hard working people.

JEALOUSY AMONG AN ELDER'S WIVES

Hatred among co-wives arose, as is common to all women, from jealousy. A man wants to marry many wives to make his name well known but a woman wants her husband for herself. Since women could not prevent men from marrying more than one wife the only thing left to them was to try and become their husband's favourite. That is why women always tried to care for their husbands by giving them good food. When a man killed an animal he divided the meat among all his wives. The women would then cook this meat as a flavouring for porridge and send it to the man's sitting place. Many people would come to sit with the man and wait for food. So often he would not eat this food sent to his place or at any rate he would not eat much of it. The wife who wished to attract him to herself would choose a good piece of meat, cook it well, and make porridge to go with it sufficient for one man. After that, if he passed near her hut, she would say, 'ee sir, won't you come and see my drying shelf (or some other thing) which has fallen to pieces?' When he entered her hut she would then say, 'sit down and drink some water.' So she would give him the little delicious food. Sometimes she would send a boy to him to ask him to come and have a look at something of hers going bad. The man would eat his food and then he would bear this wife in mind. Next time he went hunting, if he killed something like a guinea-fowl, or if somebody gave him a piece of meat, he would bring it home tied in a small bundle[1] and would put it on the shelf in her granary, saying, 'you there, take my medicine over there and pound it and cook it for me.'[2]

For this reason niggardly women hated the generous ones, because the husband favoured them. When a man cultivated for his wives and the crops were abundant he would mark the wife who was sending food to his place regularly as well as keeping him in mind.

One year a man cultivated large plots of land for his wives. There was plenty of the oil-bearing gourd *kpagu* in his cultivations. One evening this man went walking round his cultivations inspecting his wives' crops. He stepped into the plot of one of them and started throwing her biggest gourds into the plot of another wife, one who used to give him food generously. While he was thus engaged the owner of the plot had come stealthily and was standing quietly by watching him at the game. Then she burst upon him, saying, 'Mbazu, man what is this?' While she was making a lot of fuss and noise he quietly walked away, not speaking a word, with his spear over his shoulder. This woman went home and was quarrelling and complaining bitterly. When Mbazu returned the

1. So that his other wives would not have their attention drawn to it.
2. 'Medicine' in the sense of a magical substance. This is what Azande call *sanza*, double-talk.

wife into whose plot the gourds were being thrown said ironically, 'lady, do not at all mention my name. When you and your husband were throwing about your gourds did you see me there?'

When the women were quarrelling no elder bothered himself. What they said was, 'if you bother to reply to women's nagging and gossip your mouth will be tired to no purpose.' So women would quarrel and pour out their pent up anger on the man and speak to him very roughly, but he would take no notice of them. He would speak only about very important disputes. Then if one of the wives was not satisfied with his decision she would wait for a senior and influential relative of her husband and take up her case against her husband before him. A man would take his wife to the prince's court only if she refused him his marital rights.[1]

HELPING ELDERS IN THEIR CULTIVATIONS

A young man who desired to eat an elder's best food was one who would go around and if he found an elder and his wife working hard in their cultivations would say, 'oh mother, pass me that hoe for a while.' Accordingly she would hand him her hoe and go to her homestead. He would then work very hard until they finished the assigned piece of grass with the elder. In the evening they would go home and find excellent porridge with meat prepared by the woman. The elder would say casually, 'child, just eat your food young sir.' The young man would then eat the food by himself and return with the remainder to his little hut. So this elder and his wife would praise the young man's name. This young man would not pass by while the wife of the elder had something good without her giving him some of it because of his kindness. It would not be difficult if this young man wanted to marry the elder's daughter.

This is how young men gained good reputations. And so people would say, 'son of so-and-so is a very good boy.' When a good young man met an elder or his wife and he had in his hand something like a rat or a bird or some meat he would give him or her the whole thing. If he told his mother at home she would not be unhappy about it. She would just say, 'son it is good to be generous to strangers [not fellow clansmen]. You do not know what is the

1. *A ni zingi ku ti kumba*, if she was angry with the man; a euphemism for refusing him sexual congress.

future.' In those days it was more honourable to give to those who were not relatives than to kinsmen because they praised a man more. Also people used to marry from other clans, not their own.

SOME FEATURES OF ZANDE LIFE TODAY

Today our old men, the few who have survived since [King] Gbudwe's time, shake their heads and groan at our ways. The old authority of the elder over his family and the obligations towards blood-brothers, the clan, and in-laws are no longer what they were. Our mania for new ways, which we embrace immediately, has brought our morals very low.

Our villages are now organized for us. This started immediately after Gbudwe's death. We do not have to live by clans now. Members of the same clan may live in villages miles and sometimes a hundred miles apart. A man leaves one village for another as he pleases. Homesteads have not changed in structure though the huts and granaries are diminutive and less impressive, so the old men tell us. There are organized cash crops to grow and a man has neither the time nor the reason for building large huts and granaries. People do not harvest so much millet and groundnuts as they used to.

The old notion of *aparanga* [young men] is a legend to us. Young boys go to school today and the majority do not go beyond the elementary stage in education. They become labourers, houseboys and so forth. The few who return to the villages and those who do not go to school at all live as they wish. From the age of fifteen onwards a boy can marry and build a home of his own. He can buy a hoe, and axe, etc., and does not have to depend on anybody for these things. He can work for a few months to collect three pounds for his marriage if he has no parents or if his parents do not want to, or cannot, help him. Beyond mere advice a parent has no influence over his son's marriage. He chooses his girl and only informs his parents of his choice. The parents of daughters have a tottering authority over the choice of husbands for their girls. A strong-willed girl will marry whomsoever she likes. The decision now rests with the young girl and boy. When they have an understanding between them the law backs them and parents must accept their decision with good grace.

Husbands and Wives and Lovers and Families

The unmarried youth suffers and misses little. He can grow enough food (unless he is lazy) on his allotted plot. He can easily buy the necessary implements if his parents do not give him any, which is anyhow a rare case. If his mother is alive he may give her some of his produce occasionally though he will take most of his meals with her. If his parents are dead or far off he can cook for himself since the old stigma against such practices was buried long ago. The girls stay with their parents until they are married and today a girl may have as many as five husbands before she settles finally with the sixth, if ever she does settle.

Parents may extract fines in the courts from lusty young men if they catch them [with their daughters] but young people seem to be able to outwit their parents these days. The rigid rules, the custom and the punishments that were a check on both boys and girls have given way to apathy and easy-going.

The young men who stay in the villages have a growing difficulty in securing wives for themselves: the girls drift to the towns to seek means of buying cotton prints either by marrying employees of all sorts or living loosely. A young man's kindness to the old, his generosity in giving meat and other things to the wife of an elder in the hope of securing her goodwill when he asks for her daughter in marriage, is of no material benefit to him since the choice rests with the daughter and not with the mother. No wonder that no young man is now seen in the cultivations of an elder lending a hand. Anyhow he has his own plot to attend to.

Between 1945 and 1955 many thinking Azande were horrified to note that in a market-place where there might be some two hundred women, babies could be counted on one hand. The old people and the literate Azande discussed the matter but no concerted effort was made to bring it to the notice of the semi-literate, the detribalized, and the irresponsible and the indifferent Azande. After the 1956 Sudan Census it was concluded by the experts that by 1980 the Zande population would have shrunk from 200,000 to 50,000, a very alarming estimate, if the prevalent birth- and death-rates continued. It appears that though the death-rate shows no signs of dropping in the countryside, it is falling in the towns and the birth-rate seems to be climbing very slowly.

We used to think of wealth in terms of food. Today people have a half-empty granary instead of the two or three full ones of the old days. Many [traditional] crops have been displaced by cash crops, and time has been shared between the food and the cash crops. Besides, a lot of the food flows to the towns to feed the workers and employees. Many new commodities are constantly being adopted and our mania for change flourishes.

Visits to relatives and in-laws persist but as the idea of blood-brothers has almost vanished so have visits to them declined. Unfaithfulness is rife as the old forms of punishment for it have been replaced by 'progressive' forms consisting of a light fine, then a little while ago of six months imprisonment for both parties and a fine on the man, which is given to the husband. As few husbands can bear a separation of that kind from their women they accept the fine of three pounds in the 'chiefs' court' and go home. This year, I gather, the punishment is a year of hard labour for both parties and a ten pounds fine for the man. I have mentioned these degrees of punishment to illustrate the gravity of the matter. Widows and widowers still have to leave their homesteads with nothing after the death of their spouses and must start afresh in some other locality. The abstention from various kinds of food and sexual congress are no longer observed. We aptly ask, 'are there widows these days?' The period of mourning has been cut by almost half, but it must be formally terminated with a feast and the anointing of the body with oil. But the widow rarely marries a relative of her dead husband. She prefers a change, which means that the respect for marriage ties has dwindled in strength. The feuding among co-wives has become more fierce as a fair distribution of money income has surpassed those of the husband's labour and favours in importance. Division of bridewealth among brothers is not so important now that a young man can earn three pounds for his marriage and does not have to depend on his sister's bridewealth for his own marriage. Besides, marriages break up more often than before. So nobody is enthusiastic about money which you spend today and is demanded back tomorrow.

The Avongara [ruling clan] have had to stand by while their prerogatives have been slipping out of their hands. Their power over the minds of their subjects has been broken by what I might crudely call enlightenment but more because the dreadful arbitrary punishment for disrespect to princes has vanished to be replaced by a lighter one set down in law. A prince's cultivations are worked unwillingly by forced labour. A man offers a leg of a big animal to the prince because the law says so and when he cannot conceal his kill. A prince's powers as a judge are limited by what are called Zande Standing Orders, fashioned according to local custom. A prince's wife is no longer a special kind of woman and the ordinary Zande may marry from the same family as the prince and he often does so. The Zande commoners have a profound contempt for Vongara daughters because of their love of incest, and they marry them with little enthusiasm and with the feeling that they will not be faithful or make good housewives. So they are divorced on the strength of shaky suspicion. There are of course many good wives among them but the shadow of incest follows them to the grave.

You know, women are better off than men in our time, for today a woman does not depend on a man for all her possessions. All the crops which are cultivated, such as eleusine and cassava, are at her disposal. She cooks some for the daily meals, and she brews beer, such as eleusine beer (*gbangara*) and distils arrack. Really boys I think that today women get more money than men. An industrious woman earns money every day from liquor of one sort or another, and she gives some of it to her husband to help him to pay his tax and to buy his clothes. I tell you boys, a man who does not know any craft such as weaving mats, sieves and winnowing baskets, carving wooden mortars, and making cane seats, is dependent on his wife for what he possesses. Then when they quarrel she will say all she has been keeping on her mind: 'What are you, since I am the one who has been keeping you in money? If I get angry with you now and leave you, you will be as poor as a dog.' But there are many people who get their wealth not only by cultivating cotton but also by earning money by their various crafts such as carving wooden mortars, forging metal in the forge and weaving mats and making cane seats. Those people can buy bicycles just like government employees.

HOMESTEADS OF MARRIED MEN

An elder would build huts for each of his wives in turn thus: a sleeping-hut, a granary, and a kitchen-hut. Then he would build a hut for himself, the man's hut. Those wives who had no kitchens would be cooking in the sleeping huts or under the granaries while waiting for their kitchens to be built.

The elder would build a wall-less hut in the centre of the courtyard for his male visitors. In front of it was a fireplace for morning and evening fires for the men to sit round. Sweeping the fireplace and kindling the fire was the duty of the most junior wife. Often the young boys performed this duty in the evening, but in the morning she started the fire and put a pot of water near it to warm up so that the elder could wash his face with it when he came out of his sleeping hut. She would put *nzawa* leaves near the pot for him to rub his face with them [after washing it]. The most junior wife used to dry his tobacco and keep his pipe.

VISITING IN-LAWS

When a man decided to visit his in-laws he would say to his wife 'you there, today I am going to visit my mother [in-law]. People don't hide things at the side of the path when going to the home of in-laws, so I don't know the day I shall return.'[1] After she had put together some gifts for her mother he would set forth.

When a man was going to his in-laws he felt very happy because when he got there he would eat many good things at the hands of his mother-in-law. He would drink beer freely there, and he would sleep in their best hut. No child could go anywhere near the hut in which the son-in-law was lodged. No child could eat with him from the same dish. Only the very small children could be compelled by him to assist him in finishing the food prepared for him. Whenever a child was drawing anywhere near to him people would cry out 'hey you! Get away from a person. Why can't you walk far away from a person?'[2] The in-law would protest mildly 'it doesn't matter mother because he is only a little child.' To which the mother would reply 'no son, that is how a child happens to grow up with bad manners.' But an in-law would sit and converse with his big brothers-in-law and sisters-in-law. A son-in-law could joke with the younger sisters of his wife, because he would say 'you are the overflow channels of my water-hole.'[3] But he

1. A person has no need to hide food at the side of a path because there will be plenty for him at the home of his in-laws; and he cannot say how many days he may wish to stay there and enjoy it.
2. It is proper for a guest to call a small child of the home to come and share his meal with him. As the meal is likely to be a specially good one a child might be tempted to hover nearby.
3. In certain circumstances, should a wife die she may be replaced by a sister.

greatly respected the elder sisters of his wife because they were like his mother-in-law.

This generosity to the son-in-law has something behind it. He had to do many good things for all his in-laws in return. The in-laws dug the graves of the dead kin of their wives and buried them. They heaped a memorial of stones upon the grave. When they were carrying out such duties they were lavishly entertained with food and drink. Whenever a man went to the home of his in-laws he would get up early in the morning and go to the cultivations with his in-laws. If his mother-in-law's sleeping hut, granary or kitchen-hut was dilapidated he at once set about repairing it. In addition, his father-in-law could say casually one evening by the fire 'my son, I am being badly beaten by rain.' The following morning the son-in-law would simply ask for an axe and would dive into the bush to cut the poles for a hut or a granary.

The most popular son-in-law with his wife's people was one who was never shy. A son-in-law who could bounce into the home and run at once to his mother-in-law and say 'mother what shall I eat? Haven't you prepared a little beer? Mother, your daughter at home is suffering terribly from lack of groundnuts' and so on. This is the son-in-law his female in-laws would cry out about, saying 'he is no good.' But really he was the kind of man they liked. If he found beer in the home of his in-laws he would take it for himself and drink it, and they would leave him to it.

A good son-in-law was generous to his in-laws. He was not lazy nor reluctant to work for them, and he visited them often. Then if the wife of this son-in-law got annoyed and ran to their home her father would chase her back to her husband's home.

SETTLEMENTS[1] IN THE PAST

In the old days people used to live by clans.[2] They usually built their homesteads along streams. A settlement would start in this

1. The word translated 'settlement' is *gbaria*. The Azande used to live in widely dispersed homesteads and not in villages. In the Sudan they were forced by the Anglo-Egyptian Administration, for protection against sleeping sickness, to live in roadside villages called *agbaria* because they were of the shape of the traditional hunting areas of that name.
2. What is meant here is that a man and his sons and younger brothers and perhaps some other near patrilineal kinsmen made their homes along the same stream.

way: an influential elder would consult the poison oracle about his going to live by a certain stream. Then he would go with his wives and children to live near this stream. There were normally no other homesteads near that stream. After establishing a homestead and building huts for his wives he would choose a good stretch of ground for cultivations, again after consulting the poison oracle.

His sons, youths, would build their huts near their father's homestead. Small children would sleep in their mothers' huts. After this, his grown-up and married brothers and other relatives would consult the poison oracle and follow him. Some of his younger blood-brothers and in-laws would join him after consulting the poison oracle. So homesteads would spread thick along the stream. The first elder would be the leader in this new community. Among his kinsmen, blood-brothers and in-laws some would be married men with several wives together with young men and small children.

VISITING RELATIVES

Young men, and women too, used to pay visits a lot in the dry season, and in the rainy season also, to their senior relations and eat good things in their homes. But when an elder decided to pay a visit to an elder like himself he would take a young son or his latest wife to accompany him. If the relative's home was far they would spend one or two days on the way. They would sleep in the home of a relative or that of a blood-brother. When they arrived at the home of their relative the people of the home rejoiced exceedingly. The master of the household would order his wives to prepare food for his relative.

Whenever there were visitors in a home small boys were not allowed to go anywhere near them at meal times.

If the important relative spent many days they would brew red eleusine beer for him. He would then invite elders who neighboured his relative to come and drink with him at night. When he was returning he was offered many gifts, such as spears and beautiful knives.

Husbands and Wives and Lovers and Families

A MAN AND HIS SWEETHEART IN HIS HUT

Woman: 'what crooked hut is this thing? Who built this thing which can easily tumble down on people in rain? Haeee [laugh], they think they have built a hut!'

Man: 'can you build one yourself? Don't you know I did it hurriedly? If you had come I would have built a fine hut for you and a granary and a kitchen-hut near it.'

Woman: 'do I come before you build them? Or do I come to see all those things ready? Ha! Take your hand away from my breasts. Why don't you go after those who keep on abusing me for your sake?'

Man: 'leave off that silly talk of yours. Since I met you do I speak with other girls again?'

Woman: 'I will slap your mouth with that rubbish you are speaking. Was it not you I saw the other day playing with Mbazu's daughter? That behaviour of yours, one of these days I will pinch your ear for your lusting after women.'

Man: 'it is not right to accuse a person falsely, child. If you take seriously my just flirting with girls you trouble yourself for nothing. It is you in fact for whose sake men said they would kill me; but now if I see a youth speaking to you I will jump on him immediately.'

Woman: 'hiii, what people speak to me, as I am not one for young men's nonsense? Haa, is it not I who abuse the young men around here?'

Man: 'that is what you are telling me now, but when you see one dressed well as a townsman [employee of Europeans] with coins tinkling in his pockets are you sure you will not jump up here to land over there [far off]?'

Woman: 'you say what you will do when you see your prostitute [from town], then you won't even look at me again. You are talking about money to me, who said I care about money? It is only the person I love that I speak with.'

Man: 'such as whom? eee!'

Woman: 'like the man who is asking me now.'

Man: 'o baby [in American slang sense], these are things I like to hear from you. Please just draw a little closer. . . .'

Woman: 'what am I moving near you to do? Is this not the way men deceive a person, and when you marry one of them does he not begin to beat you and ill-treat you like an animal? The habits of men, hai! At first he is always tender with you, but when you have been some time with him he turns you into a dog.'

Man: 'o my sister e, my clan are strangers to ill-treating women. Why should I beat a woman, is she a man like me?'

Woman: 'soo, as if I did not see men and their wives before; is this how you would be deceiving me?'

Man: 'do you think people all have the same character?'

Woman: 'do men's habits differ at all? Some follow their wives to the water-hole and also to where they fetch firewood, and some cut meat for their wives into the pot [out of meanness].'

Man: 'men who are greedy for food are shameless who enter the kitchen after their wives to see what sort of food the wife is cooking. We sons of elders do not know that sort of shamelessness. What exactly can make me follow a woman? My wife will wander to return and find me in the home. My father didn't know how to follow his wives, so after whom would I take the following of women?'

Woman: 'o sir, there are also some men who do not bear their in-laws in mind. The mother of a child suffers much with it [in bearing it], you know!'

Man: 'wait and see my character as we are going to be married. The only thing I much dislike is letting me suffer hunger. If a woman exasperates me with this it would spoil our home life.'

Woman: 'hiii, but who is marrying you anyway?'

Man: 'o child, madam, are you saying that so I may go and hang myself?'

Woman: 'those whom people hang their necks about, do they look like me sir?'

Man: 'leave off that talk child. What nonsense are you now saying like that [are you exasperating me with]?'

Woman: 'you there o, take your hand off me so that I may return home to do a bit of work.'

Man: 'huu, you will not return today. Is it not late now? You will return tomorrow. We sit [make love] first.'

Woman: 'o my brother, my father would be angry.'

Man: 'then we will converse first, after that I will accompany you in case an animal might seize you on the way alone.'

Husbands and Wives and Lovers and Families

YOUTH AND GIRL AT A DANCE

Girl: 'my brother, give me what is left of the cigarette. Where are you drinking beer today?'

Youth: 'if when I have given you tobacco your husband attacks me what shall I do since I don't like fights at a dance?'

Girl: 'do people as ugly as me get husbands sir? What you are trying to say is that you are scared of your wife. Hii, let me go my way or a woman may come and stab me with her knife.'

Youth: 'haa, come here and get your tobacco child. Who told you I am married? In fact I often wonder where I will find a nice girl like you to propose to her, and if she rejects me, well, that will be just too bad.'

Girl: 'eeee, what about those girls I see returning from your home in the morning, and how about those you were dancing with here [just now]?'

Youth: 'oh no, women don't approach the doorway of my hut. . . .'

Girl: 'does your mother get angry with them?'

Youth: 'not at all, it is only that I do not like the crazy girls of these days. I want somebody's daughter who has a sense of shame. Those I was dancing with are my elder brothers' wives and my maternal uncle's wives.'

Girl: 'all right sir. Then I am going to dance my dance if you please.'

Youth: 'wait a bit. Aren't you tired of dancing? It is past midnight. Come let us go and leave the dance to the dancers.'

Girl: 'where are we to go?'

Youth: 'to my home of course.'

Girl: 'no sir, I don't go to men's homes by night. If I go with you now at night and my brothers look for me and can't find me what will I tell them tomorrow?'

Youth: 'you tell them you went with your [girl] friends to their home because you were sleepy.'

Girl: 'they will ask why in that case I didn't just go to our home. If you are interested in me, come to our home tomorrow.'

Youth: 'if I go to your home how shall I be able to talk to you, since I will be afraid of your brothers. It should be for you to visit my sisters and then I will be able to talk with you. Isn't it so?'

Girl: 'it is so. So I will go there tomorrow at mid-day or in the evening. I am hoeing my mother's cultivations first in the morning.'

Youth: 'better come in the evening because at mid-day we shall be hunting. Is that settled?'

Girl: 'yes friend, now stop bothering me.'

Youth: 'come then, let us go and drink beer here where my fathers are in the hut.'

GIRLS TALK ABOUT MEN

A: 'my mother's child, Naapenesi said you went the other day to that place.'

B: 'to where?'

A: 'he, are you saying you don't know the place I mean?'

B: 'of a truth, God I don't know the place you are thinking about. But there are many places I am thinking about; which one exactly are you asking me about?'

A: 'hu my sister, didn't Fatiro meet us the other day about twelve o'clock and tell you to come in the cool of the evening to take some tobacco?'

B: 'my friend so! Is that the silly place you are talking big about to me now? My affairs have nothing to do with Fatiro, my younger sister.'

A: 'eee my sister, you were pretty eager to agree with his suggestion, do you not mean to go?'

B: 'by God girl, what that man did to me, if a man did it to you I don't think you would even return his greeting again.'

A: 'what did he do to you sister?'

B: 'It was like this. He met me with another girl, my maternal uncle's daughter. This was in the evening. He told us that there was beer in his home and that I should go there when people retired for the night so that we might drink it. When the time he arranged came I asked this daughter of my uncle to accompany me because it was very dark that night. So, my sister, when we arrived there we found the man playing with his girl friends in his hut.'

A: 'I suppose that after that he didn't give you much of a welcome?'

B: 'As a matter of fact he came out, and after greeting me he told us that the only place to sit was inside.'

A: 'did you enter the hut and see those women?'

B: 'yes. My first idea was to rush at them inside and pull those daughters of dogs outside by their legs, and after that to break all the gourds from which they were drinking alcohol. Only that daughter of my uncle who went with me prevented me. That is why we only entered and after seeing him with his women we left them there doing what was fit for their persons and returned that very night.'

A: 'who were these women? Did you know them? What were they like?'

B: 'I knew one, the same one you said was abusing me the other day to Yangatayo during the dance at his home, Nasimindi. I have seen the other one with this woman of his. They say she is the daughter of her mother's younger sister who has recently come from the Congo.'

A: 'what an astonishing thing, how can one man take two women into his hut?'

B: 'don't ask me. Perhaps the other one only accompanied her as my uncle's daughter accompanied me.'

A: 'o mother! God, when I hear something like that I feel that it might have happened to me. That night we would certainly all have been lacking, as I am Nameneti.'

B: 'eee, my sister I must not be told that. I kept my temper on account of that daughter of my uncle who went with me, for it is not good to go with a friend and start trouble which involves her.'

A: 'ee, my younger sister, it is the habit of people of those parts to be proud to their sisters whom they grew up with. What makes them be like this?'

B: 'I don't think of that my younger sister. I have found another young man of mine who is handsome and smooth.'

A and B: 'ha ha ha eeee, wawayeee [girls' laughter].'

LOVE AFFAIRS

Firstly, with regard to unmarried girls. Making love to unmarried girls was not considered a bad thing for young men. Young men went to dances and could offer tobacco to their sweethearts and dance with them without reserve or shame [their fathers pretending not to notice]. On their part the girls could give anything to their friends. A girl would beg her mother to give her a chicken and when it was given she would cook it [in oil] and take it to her friend in his little hut. If she found good meat she would prepare a meal with it for her lover. If her mother brewed beer she would fill a gourd with it and take it to him. He himself, if he obtained good meat or an ornament he would quickly give it to his sweetheart. No girl would eat anything while her lover was looking on.

A certain girl went to her lover's hut but she did not find him in the hut. But when she looked around the hut she found some boiled manioc and groundnut paste which had been brought to him by his sister. As she was hungry she began to eat it hurriedly and was choked by it, but when she looked for water she could not find any; so she struggled and died from manioc and groundnut paste. When her lover returned he found only her dead body.

Secondly, sexual relations with married women. One's death was not far off if one went after married women; but many young men became lovers of married women because many elders had young women as their wives. The lover of an elder's wife often ate of the elder's best food. When an elder killed an animal, this woman would cook some of the best meat for her lover. If she went fishing she would select the best fish to cook them for her lover. Most of this food was hidden on the path to where the wife drew water in places known to the lovers. So boys and young men sometimes followed their father's wives secretly to the place of drawing water. When a woman brought out food from the water-pot and hid it in the fork of a tree these children would know its whereabouts. As soon as she was out of sight the boys would eat the food, and the lover would be disappointed.

Making love to people's wives was the cause in the past of mutilating people's hands, lips, ears and eye-lids [and genitals]. When a man knew a youth had an affair with his wife he would call together his male kinsmen and they would go stealthily and seize the young man and cut off his hands, ears and lips. Then they would cut off his genitals so that he would not meddle with people's wives again.

Lastly, sexual relations with wives of kinsmen. A man could become the lover of the wives of his relatives, even of his father's wife; but I have not been told that a man ever mutilated a relative

on account of a woman. They would however naturally hate
each other. It seems that the husband said 'I married for them. It
does not matter. After all, when I die one of them will marry
her.'

TWO WOMEN GOSSIPING

A: 'my dear girl, from where have you lost your way to come here?
You hide your face at the end of the village and one would think
you had gone beyond the river Were [a great distance].'

B: 'sister I have been all the time at home. Do you think at the
time of shamelessness in this village I want to show my face?'

A: 'what has happened up there again? You have indeed got a
reputation. I haven't been to your parts recently. My sister, tell me
the news.'

B: ' "have you heard this" causes people death these days. I
detest bringing up people's affairs.'

A: 'my sister, do you mean that it is untrue what has actually
taken place and everybody is aware of it? Gossip is taking things
out of your stomach [heart] and attributing it to people's names.
What has spread all over the place, if you tell your sister, is it
"have you heard this?" I myself do not like snatching up people's
affairs and making them public. A person tells me a secret and
listens afterwards in vain without hearing a trace of it again from
other people.'

B: 'o sister, I didn't accuse you of spreading lies or being indiscreet. Are you new to me? Look you, they say Kurame's wife
has carried all the soaked manioc belonging to Kpanga's wife from
the stream bank.'

A: 'ha! That woman is really a disgrace! Why steal manioc?
Is there no mere manioc around her home? Look you, if we
strengthen our limbs for bearing tiny weak children we should also
strengthen our hands to cultivate for their mouths.'

B: 'when Kpanga's wife didn't find her manioc on the bank she
followed the footprints of Kurame's wife until she reached the
home and found her big long manioc roots there in a basket.
When she inquired about it Kurame and his wife rose against her;
can you imagine such dreadful trouble? They took up the case to
the headmen but they are still looking for witnesses.'

A: 'such a husband as sides with his thief of a wife I consider to be a thief like his wife.'

B: 'who do you imagine Kurame to be? Who do you think stole Banga's groundnuts last year if it was not Kurame himself?'

A: 'o sister, are you speaking the truth?'

B: 'do I go about my dear! I sit in my place and hear all my news. Have you not heard that Baiwo's wife has revolted against him?'

A: 'speak it out sister! Has she seen another one again? Oh that girl, she has always been fond of going from one man to another!'

B: 'my dear, do I go about! They say Baimeyo "has come out for her" and is vastly enjoying himself with her.'

A: 'is that why Muka's daughter left him?'

B: 'do you think that all these animals Baiwo has been killing this year, it is he who has been eating the best part of them? It has now reached a climax and she has decided it is better to break from Baiwo and marry Baimeyo.'

A: 'despite all the things Baiwo has done for that arch-backed woman! That boy really loves a woman. Really the man for whom she can reject Baiwo is he Baimeyo? We women seem to have our eyes on the soles of our feet! Does she know Baimeyo's meanness?'

B: 'let us wait and see the bottom of the elephant with the breadfruit![1] You will again see her reject that bald-headed Baimeyo.'

1. A well-known Zande proverb. An elephant swallows the big fruit of the breadfruit tree whole. It will have some difficulty in excreting it. It may have overreached itself. If someone is attempting to do something which is perhaps beyond his ability this proverb is used: let us wait and see what happens.

Index

Adultery, 21–4, 49, 66, 77–8, 82, 85, 109–10, 110–11, 119–20, 127–33, 134–5, 136, 184, 194–5
Aunt (paternal), 86; (maternal uncle's wife), 86–7

Barreness, 53
Birth, 22–6
Blessings, 36, 78, 101, 156
Blood-brotherhood, 14, 30, 96–7, 182, 184, 188
Bridewealth, 24, 27, 28–30, 32, 33, 34, 35, 36, 59, 60, 90–1, 143–4, 172–3, 182, 184

Children, 19–20, 25–6, 47–8, 107
Conception (and pregnancy), 19–24
Co-wives, 48–50, 50–1
Curses, 78–81, 97–8, 102

Dances, 114–17
Dreams, 122

Elders, 30–2, 47–8, 75–8, 79, 104, 129, 130, 132, 133, 150, 153–4, 155, 176–83, 185–6, 188–90, 194

Ghosts, 26, 81, 89, 96, 99–100, 100–1, 102, 173
Girls, their opinion of men, 192–3

Husbands and wives, 34, 35, 47–8, 48–52, 54–8, 58–60, 60–5, 65–6, 67–72, 144–62, 165–76

Incest, 107–8, 122, 135, 185
In-law behaviour, 85–6, 89–92, 98–99, 103–5

Kinship, 87–9

Lesbianism, 123–5
Lovers, 50, 111–13, 117–18, 118–119, 189–90, 191–2, 193–5

Magic (medicines), 13, 25, 52, 55, 58, 60, 62, 64, 78, 80, 96, 99, 100–1, 115–16, 129, 130, 132, 136, 145, 164, 176, 180
Marriage, 13–14, 26–33, 34, 35–6, 37–47, 50
Masturbation, 113–14
Meals, 47–8, 76
Midwives, 24–5
Mutilation, 24, 133–4, 194–5

Oracles, 13
Orphans, 75

Poison oracle, 13, 21, 26, 29, 36, 53, 63, 72, 80, 82, 83–4, 86, 93–4, 135, 155, 163, 171–2, 188

Rubbing-board oracle, 23, 36, 68, 72, 100

Sisters, 81–4; sister's son, 84
Suicides, 105–6

Vengeance, 134–5

Widows (and widowers), 66–7, 72–3, 168–170, 184
Witchcraft, 13, 26, 29, 59, 66, 68, 75, 94, 96, 99, 101, 102, 104, 132, 134–5, 142, 145, 146, 156, 160, 162–5, 167–8, 173
Witch-doctors, 162–5
Women, work, 60; men's opinion of, 125–6